FIX-IT and FORGET-IT®

SLOW COOKER CROWD PLEASERS
FOR THE AMERICAN SUMMER

150 FAVORITE RECIPES
FOR POTLUCKS, PARTIES, AND FAMILY GATHERINGS

HOPE COMERFORD
PHOTOS BY BONNIE MATTHEWS

Good Books®

New York, New York

Good Books books may be purchased in bulk at special discounts for sales promotion, corporate gifts, fund-raising, or educational purposes. Special editions can also be created to specifications. For details, contact the Special Sales Department, Good Books, 307 West 36th Street, 11th Floor, New York, NY 10018 or info@skyhorsepublishing.com.

Good Books is an imprint of Skyhorse Publishing, Inc.®, a Delaware corporation.

Visit our website at www.goodbooks.com.

10 9 8 7 6 5 4 3 2 1

Library of Congress Cataloging-in-Publication Data is available on file.

Cover design by Jane Sheppard
Cover photo by Bonnie Matthews

Print ISBN: 978-1-68099-377-6
Ebook ISBN: 978-1-68099-403-2

Printed in China

To my amazing husband: you're my biggest fan and supporter.
I love you more and more every day.
"Every love story is beautiful, but ours is my favorite."

Table of Contents

Welcome to Fix-It and Forget-It Slow Cooker Crowd Pleasers for the American Summer!

During the summer, heating up your kitchen with your oven is the last thing you need! Summer is when you want to be outside, going to the park, spending the day with your family, and being out and about . . . not standing over the stove or grill. We've got you covered with recipes you can bring to picnics, church gatherings, barbecues, or put on your family table. If you're not already using your slow cooker during the summer months, you're missing out! Your mouth will be watering over the delicious recipes in this book, and you'll soon be using your slow cooker almost exclusively during those summer months.

Choosing a Slow Cooker

Not all slow cookers are created equal . . . or work equally as well for everyone!

Those of us who use slow cookers frequently know we have our own preferences when it comes to which slow cooker we choose to use. For instance, I love my programmable slow cooker, but there are many programmable slow cookers I've tried that I've strongly disliked. Why? Because some go by increments of 15 or 30 minutes and some go by 4, 6, 8, or 10 hours. I dislike those restrictions, but I have family and friends who don't mind them at all! I am also pretty brand-loyal when it comes to my manual slow cookers because I've had great success with those and have had unsuccessful moments with slow cookers of other brands. So, which slow cooker(s) is/are best for your household?

It really depends on how many people you're feeding and if you're away from the house for long periods of time. Here are my recommendations:

For 2–3 person household	3–5 quart slow cooker
For 4–5 person household	5–6 quart slow cooker
For a 6+ person household	6½–7 quart slow cooker

Large slow cooker advantages/disadvantages:

Advantages:
- You can fit a loaf pan or a baking dish into a 6- or 7-quart, depending on the shape of your cooker. That allows you to make bread or cakes, or even smaller quantities of main dishes. (Take your favorite baking dish and loaf pan along when you shop for a cooker to make sure they'll fit inside.)
- You can feed large groups of people, or make larger quantities of food, allowing for leftovers, or meals, to freeze.

Disadvantages:
- They take up more storage room.
- They don't fit as neatly into a dishwasher.
- If your crock isn't ⅔–¾ full, you may burn your food.

Small slow cooker advantages/disadvantages:

Advantages:
- They're great for lots of appetizers, for serving hot drinks, for baking cakes straight in the crock, and for dorm rooms or apartments.
- Great option for making recipes of smaller quantities.

Disadvantages:
- Food in smaller quantities tends to cook more quickly than larger amounts. So keep an eye on it.
- Chances are, you won't have many leftovers. So, if you like to have leftovers, a smaller slow cooker may not be a good option for you.

My recommendation:

Have at least two slow cookers; one around 3 to 4 quarts and one 6 quarts or larger. A third would be a huge bonus (and a great advantage to your cooking repertoire!). The advantage of having at least a couple is you can make a larger variety of recipes. Also, you can make at least two or three dishes at once for a whole meal.

Manual vs. Programmable

If you are gone for only six to eight hours a day, a manual slow cooker might be just fine for you. If you are gone for more than eight hours during the day, I would highly recommend purchasing a programmable slow cooker that will switch to Warm when the cook time you set is up. It will allow you to cook a wider variety of recipes.

The two I use most frequently are my 4-quart manual slow cooker and my 6½-quart programmable slow cooker. I like that I can make smaller portions in my 4-quart slow cooker on days I don't need or want leftovers, but I also love how my 6½-quart slow cooker can accommodate whole chickens, turkey breasts, hams, or big batches of soups. I use them both often.

Get to know your slow cooker . . .

Plan a little time to get acquainted with your slow cooker. Each slow cooker has its own personality—just like your oven (and your car). Plus, many new slow cookers cook hotter and faster than earlier models. I think that with all of the concern for food safety, the slow cooker manufacturers have amped up their settings so that "High," "Low," and "Warm" are all higher temperatures than in the older models. That means they cook hotter—and therefore, faster—than the first slow cookers. The beauty of these little machines is that they're supposed to cook low and slow. We count on that when we flip the switch in the morning before we leave the house for ten hours or so. So, because none of us knows what kind of temperament our slow cooker has until we try it out, nor how hot it cooks—don't assume anything. Save yourself a disappointment and make the first recipe in your new slow cooker on a day when you're at home. Cook it for the shortest amount of time the recipe calls for. Then, check the food to see if it's done. Or if you start smelling food that seems to be finished, turn off the cooker and rescue your food.

Also, all slow cookers seem to have a "hot spot," which is of great importance to know, especially when baking with your slow cooker. This spot may tend to burn food in that area if you're not careful. If you're baking directly in your slow cooker, I recommend covering the "hot spot" with some foil.

Take notes . . .

Don't be afraid to make notes in your cookbook. It's yours! Chances are, it will eventually get passed down to someone in your family and they will love and appreciate all of your musings. Take note of which slow cooker you used and exactly how long it took to cook the recipe. The next time you make it, you won't need to try to remember. Apply what you learned to the next recipes you make in your cooker. If another recipe says it needs to cook 7–9 hours, and you've discovered your slow cooker cooks on the faster side, cook that recipe for 6–6½ hours and then check it. You can always cook a recipe longer—but you can't reverse things if it's overdone.

Get creative . . .

If you know your morning is going to be hectic, prepare everything the night before, take it out so the crock warms up to room temperature when you first get up in the morning, then plug it in and turn it on as you're leaving the house.

If you want to make something that has a short cook time and you're going to be gone longer than that, cook it the night before and refrigerate it for the next day. Warm it up when you get home. Or, cook those recipes on the weekend when you know you'll be home and eat them later in the week.

Slow-Cooking Tips and Tricks and Other Things You May Not Know

- Slow cookers tend to work best when they're ⅔ to ¾ of the way full. You may need to increase the cooking time if you've exceeded that amount, or reduce it if you've put in less than that. If you're going to exceed that limit, it would be best to reduce the recipe, or split it between two slow cookers. (Remember how I suggested owning at least two or three slow cookers?)
- Keep your veggies on the bottom. That puts them in more direct contact with the heat. The fuller your slow cooker, the longer it will take its contents to cook. Also, the more densely packed the cooker's contents are, the longer they will take to cook. And finally, the larger the chunks of meat or vegetables, the more time they will need to cook.
- Keep the lid on! Every time you take a peek, you lose 20 minutes of cooking time. Please take this into consideration each time you lift the lid! I know, some of you can't help yourself and are going to lift anyway. Just don't forget to tack on 20 minutes to your cook time for each time you peeked!

- Sometimes it's beneficial to remove the lid. If you'd like your dish to thicken a bit, take the lid off during the last half hour to hour of cooking time.
- If you have a big slow cooker (7- to 8-quart), you can cook a small batch in it by putting the recipe ingredients into an ovensafe baking dish or baking pan and then placing that into the cooker's crock. First, put a trivet or some metal jar rings on the bottom of the crock, and then set your dish or pan on top of them. Or a loaf pan may "hook onto" the top ridges of the crock belonging to a large oval cooker and hang there straight and securely, "baking" a cake or quick bread. Cover the cooker and flip it on.
- The outside of your slow cooker will be hot! Please remember to keep it out of reach of children and keep that in mind for yourself as well!
- Get yourself a quick-read meat thermometer and use it! This helps remove the question of whether or not your meat is fully cooked, and helps prevent you from overcooking your meat as well.

Internal Cooking Temperatures:
- Beef—125–130°F (rare); 140–145°F (medium); 160°F (well-done)
- Pork—140–145°F (rare); 145–150°F (medium); 160°F (well-done)
- Turkey and Chicken—165°F
- Frozen meat: The basic rule of thumb is, don't put frozen meat into the slow cooker. The meat does not reach the proper internal temperature in time. This especially applies to thick cuts of meat! Proceed with caution!
- Add fresh herbs 10 minutes before the end of the cooking time to maximize their flavor.
- If your recipe calls for cooked pasta, add it 10 minutes before the end of the cooking time if the cooker is on High; 30 minutes before the end of the cooking time if it's on Low. Then the pasta won't get mushy.
- If your recipe calls for sour cream or cream, stir it in 5 minutes before the end of the cooking time. You want it to heat but not boil or simmer.

Approximate Slow-Cooker Temperatures (Remember, each slow cooker is different):
- High—212°F–300°F
- Low—170°F–200°F
- Simmer—185°F
- Warm—165°F

Cooked and dried bean measurements:
- 16-oz. can, drained = about 1¾ cups beans
- 19-oz. can, drained = about 2 cups beans
- 1 lb. dried beans (about 2½ cups) = 5 cups cooked beans

Appetizers, Snacks & Drinks

Honey Barbecue Meatballs

Hope Comerford, Clinton Township, MI

Makes 15–20 servings

Prep. Time: 15 minutes ❧ *Cooking Time: 4 hours, 15 minutes* ❧ *Ideal slow-cooker size: 3–4 qt.*

Meatballs:
1 lb. lean ground beef

1 egg

¾ cup panko bread crumbs

2 Tbsp. minced dry onion

1 Tbsp. garlic powder

1 tsp. salt

¼ tsp. pepper

2–3 Tbsp. olive oil

Sauce:
1 cup barbecue sauce

¼ cup honey

2 tsp. Worcestershire sauce

½ tsp. salt

⅛ tsp. pepper

1. Mix the meatball ingredients (except the oil) together and form into small meatballs.

2. In a large skillet, heat the olive oil over medium-high heat. Brown the meatballs lightly, just until they are sealed on all sides.

3. Place the meatballs into the crock.

4. In a bowl, mix together the sauce ingredients. Pour over the meatballs.

5. Cover and cook on Low for 4 hours.

Sweet 'n Sour Meatballs

Valerie Drobel, Carlisle, PA
Sharon Hannaby, Frederick, MD

Makes 15–20 servings

Prep. Time: 10 minutes ⚓ *Cooking Time: 2–4 hours* ⚓ *Ideal slow-cooker size: 3- to 4-qt.*

12-oz. jar grape jelly

12-oz. jar chili sauce

2 1-lb. bags prepared frozen meatballs, thawed

1. Combine jelly and sauce in slow cooker. Stir well.

2. Add meatballs. Stir to coat.

3. Cover and heat on Low 4 hours, or on High 2 hours. Keep slow cooker on Low while serving.

Variation:

Instead of meatballs, use 2 1-lb. pkgs. smoked cocktail sausages.

—Krista Hershberger, Elverson, PA

TIP
If your meatballs are frozen, add another hour to the cooking time.

Chipotle Orange Barbecue Meatballs

Hope Comerford, Clinton Township, MI

Makes 12–14 servings

Prep. Time: 10 minutes & Cooking Time: 4–6 hours & Ideal slow-cooker size: 6-qt.

32-oz. pkg. frozen meatballs

28-oz. bottle sweet barbecue sauce

18-oz. jar orange marmalade

3 chipotle peppers in adobo sauce, chopped

1 Tbsp. adobo sauce

1 Tbsp. fresh minced garlic

1. Spray crock with nonstick spray, then dump meatballs in.

2. In a bowl, mix together all the remaining ingredients. Pour over the meatballs, then stir to coat.

3. Cover and cook on Low for 4–6 hours.

Barbecued Cocktail Sausages

Jena Hammond, Traverse City, MI

Makes 48–60 appetizer servings

Prep. Time: 5 minutes   ❧   Cooking Time: 4 hours   ❧   Ideal slow-cooker size: 4-qt.

4 16-oz. pkgs. little smoked cocktail sausages

18-oz. bottle barbecue sauce

1. Mix ingredients together in slow cooker.

2. Cover and cook on Low for 4 hours.

Summer "Baked" Brie

Hope Comerford, Clinton Township, MI

Makes 12 servings

Prep. Time: 10 minutes ⚮ *Cooking Time: 1–3 hours* ⚮ *Ideal slow-cooker size: 2-qt.*

¼ cup diced peaches
¼ cup diced nectarines
¼ cup rhubarb preserves
1 Tbsp. brandy
2 8-oz. brie cheese rounds

1. Combine fresh peaches, nectarines, preserves, and brandy.

2. Line crock with parchment paper.

3. Place both brie rounds in bottom of the crock, then pour the fruit mixture over the top.

4. Cover and cook on Low for 2–3 hours or High 1 hour, until brie is softened but not melted.

5. Gently lift brie out of crock by the edges of the parchment paper. Serve with crackers.

Creamy Artichoke Dip

Jessica Stoner, West Liberty, OH

Makes 7–8 cups, or 28–32 servings

Prep. Time: 15–20 minutes ♣ *Cooking Time: 1 hour* ♣ *Ideal slow-cooker size: 3-qt.*

2 14-oz. cans water-packed artichoke hearts, coarsely chopped (drain one can; stir juice from other can into Dip)

2 cups (8 oz.) shredded, low-fat part-skim mozzarella cheese

8-oz. pkg. fat-free cream cheese, softened

1 cup grated reduced-fat Parmesan cheese

½ cup shredded low-fat Swiss cheese

½ cup fat-free mayonnaise

2 Tbsp. lemon juice

2 Tbsp. fat-free plain yogurt

1 Tbsp. seasoned salt

1 Tbsp. chopped, seeded jalapeño pepper

1 tsp. garlic powder

Dippers: baked tortilla chips

1. In slow cooker, combine artichoke hearts, cheeses, mayonnaise, lemon juice, yogurt, salt, jalapeño pepper, and garlic powder.

2. Cover. Cook on Low 1 hour, or until cheeses are melted and Dip is heated through.

3. Serve with baked tortilla chips.

Variation:

Add 2 10-oz. pkgs. frozen chopped spinach, thawed and squeezed dry, to Step 1.
—Steven Lantz, Denver, CO

Spinach Dip Mexican Style

Laura Peachey, Goshen, IN

Makes 12–15 servings

Prep. Time: 15 minutes & *Cooking Time: 2–3 hours* & *Ideal slow-cooker size: 3-qt.*

10-oz. box frozen spinach, thawed and chopped

16-oz. jar salsa (I use medium)

2 cups shredded sharp cheese

8-oz. pkg. cream cheese, room temperature

1 cup Greek yogurt, room temperature

½ cup chopped black olives

2 Tbsp. lime juice

1 tsp. chili powder

1. Combine all ingredients in slow cooker.

2. Heat on Low 2–3 hours. Stir twice.

3. Serve as a dip for tortilla chips, bread cubes, or carrot and celery sticks.

White Queso Dip

Janie Steele, Moore, OK

Makes 10–12 servings

Prep. Time: 10–15 minutes ⚬ Cooking Time: 1 hour ⚬ Ideal slow-cooker size: 2-qt.

2 8-oz. pkgs. cream cheese, either regular or low-fat, softened

1 cup sour cream, either regular or low-fat

½ tsp. hot sauce

10-oz. can Ro*Tel tomatoes, your choice of hot or mild

1 tsp. cumin

4-oz. can green chilies, chopped

8-oz. pkg. grated Monterey Jack cheese, or grated Mexican cheese mix

1. Combine cream cheese, sour cream, and hot sauce in a bowl with a mixer until smooth.

2. Drain half the liquid off the tomatoes and discard.

3. Add tomatoes with half their juice, cumin, chilies, and grated cheese to creamy mixture. Stir to combine.

4. Pour mixture into slow cooker.

5. Turn to High until cheese melts, about 1 hour. Stir about every 15 minutes.

6. Turn to Low or Warm to keep dip warm while serving.

Serving suggestion:

Serve with tortilla chips.

Marilyn's Chili Con Queso

Marilyn Mowry, Irving, TX

Makes 2 cups dip

Prep. Time: 10–15 minutes ⚉ *Cooking Time: 1–2 hours* ⚉ *Ideal slow-cooker size: 1½-qt.*

1 Tbsp. chopped green peppers
1 Tbsp. chopped celery
1 Tbsp. chopped onions
2 Tbsp. diced tomatoes
2 tsp. chopped jalapeño pepper
½ cup water
¾ cup heavy cream
8 oz. Velveeta cheese, cubed
2 oz. cheddar cheese, shredded

1. Place first 5 ingredients in slow cooker. Add water.

2. Cover. Cook on High 1 hour, or until vegetables are tender.

3. Stir in cream and cheeses.

4. Reduce heat to Low. Cook until cheese is melted. Serve immediately, or keep warm on Low or Warm for hours.

Serving suggestion:

Serve with tortilla chips.

Chili Cheese Dip

Vicki Dinkel, Sharon Springs, KS

Makes 8 servings

Prep. Time: 10–15 minutes ⚜ *Cooking Time: 4 hours* ⚜ *Ideal slow-cooker size: 2-qt.*

1 onion, diced

8-oz. pkg. fat-free cream cheese, cubed

2 15-oz. cans low-fat vegetarian chili without beans

2 tsp. garlic salt

1½ cups salsa

Baked tortilla chips, for serving

1. Lightly brown onion in skillet sprayed with nonfat cooking spray. Transfer to slow cooker.

2. Stir in cream cheese, chili, garlic salt, and salsa.

3. Cover. Cook on Low 4 hours, stirring occasionally.

4. Serve with baked tortilla chips.

Prairie Fire Dip

Cheri Jantzen, Houston, TX

Makes 1¼ cups, or 10 servings

Prep. Time: 5–10 minutes ⚜ Cooking Time: 1–3 hours ⚜ Ideal slow-cooker size: 2-qt.

1 cup refried fat-free beans
(half a 15-oz. can)

½ cup shredded fat-free Monterey Jack
cheese

¼ cup water

1 Tbsp. minced onion

1 clove garlic, minced

2 tsp. chili powder

hot sauce, as desired

1. Combine all ingredients in slow cooker.

2. Cover. Cook on High 1 hour, or on Low 2–3 hours.

Serving Suggestion:

Serve with baked tortilla chips.

TIP
This recipe can easily be doubled.

Cheesy New Orleans Shrimp Dip

Kelly Amos, Pittsboro, NC

Makes 3–4 cups dip, or 24 servings

Prep. Time: 20–30 minutes ❧ *Cooking Time: 1 hour* ❧ *Ideal slow-cooker size: 2-qt.*

1 slice lean turkey bacon

3 medium-sized onions, chopped

1 clove garlic, minced

4 jumbo shrimp, peeled and deveined

1 medium-sized tomato, peeled and chopped

3 cups shredded low-fat Monterey Jack cheese

4 drops Tabasco sauce

1/8 tsp. cayenne pepper

dash black pepper

1. Cook bacon until crisp. Drain on paper towel. Cut fine.

2. Sauté onions and garlic in bacon drippings. Drain on paper towel.

3. Coarsely chop shrimp.

4. Combine all ingredients in slow cooker.

5. Cover. Cook on Low 1 hour, or until cheese is melted. Thin with milk if too thick.

Serving suggestion:

Serve with chips.

Crab Spread

Jeanette Oberholtzer, Manheim, PA

Makes 8 servings

Prep. Time: 20 minutes   ♣   Cooking Time: 4 hours   ♣   Ideal slow-cooker size: 1- to 3-qt.

½ cup mayonnaise

8 oz. cream cheese, softened

2 Tbsp. apple juice

I onion, minced

I lb. lump crabmeat, picked over to remove cartilage and shell bits

1. Mix mayonnaise, cheese, and juice in medium-sized bowl until blended.

2. Stir in onion, mixing well. Gently stir in crabmeat.

3. Place in slow cooker, cover, and cook on Low for 4 hours.

4. Dip will hold for 2 hours. Stir occasionally. Serve with snack crackers, snack bread, or crudités.

Herbed Cheese Terrine

Nancy J. Reppert, Mechanicsburg, PA

Makes 20 servings

Prep. Time: 20 minutes & Cooking Time: 3–5 hours Chilling Time: 9 hours & Ideal slow-cooker size: 6-qt.

2 8-oz. pkgs. cream cheese, room temperature

½ cup crumbled feta cheese

½ tsp. garlic powder

⅛ tsp. black pepper

½ cup plain Greek yogurt

2 eggs

2 tsp. finely grated lemon peel

½ cup chopped fresh herbs, any combination of parsley, basil, cilantro, or dill

2 green onions, thinly sliced

¼ cup minced sun-dried tomatoes, drained if oil packed

¼ cup chopped Greek black olives

red and green lettuce leaves, for serving

crackers or baguette slices, for serving

1. In a mixing bowl, beat cream cheese. Add feta, garlic powder, and black pepper and beat again.

2. Mix in yogurt, eggs, and lemon peel until just smooth.

3. Stir in herbs, onions, tomatoes, and olives.

4. Pour water in slow cooker to depth of 1–2 inches.

5. Prepare an 8-inch loaf pan by greasing it well and placing a rectangle of parchment paper on its bottom. Pour cheese mixture in prepared pan.

6. Lower pan into water in cooker—the water should come up about halfway on the pan.

7. Cover and cook on High for 3–5 hours, until center of loaf is softly set.

8. Wearing oven mitts to protect your knuckles, remove hot pan from cooker and allow to cool for 1 hour. Cover and chill for at least 8 hours.

9. Gently unmold terrine on bed of lettuce leaves on platter. Serve with crackers or baguette slices.

Italiano Spread

Nanci Keatley, Salem, OR

Makes 8 servings

Prep. Time: 15 minutes ⚓ *Cooking Time: 2–3 hours* ⚓ *Ideal slow-cooker size: 2-qt.*

2 8-oz. pkgs. cream cheese, softened
1 cup prepared pesto
3 medium tomatoes, chopped
1 cup shredded mozzarella cheese
½ cup shredded Parmesan cheese
2 Tbsp. olive oil

1. Spread cream cheese on bottom of slow cooker.

2. Spread pesto over cream cheese.

3. Add a layer of chopped tomatoes over cream cheese and pesto.

4. Sprinkle cheeses on top of tomatoes.

5. Drizzle olive oil over top.

6. Cook on Low 2–3 hours or until cheese is melted.

Serving suggestion:

Spread on crackers or slices of Italian bread.

Colorful Fruit Salsa

Joyce Shackelford, Green Bay, WI

Makes 8–10 servings

Prep. Time: 25 minutes ⚬ Cooking Time: 2 hours ⚬ Ideal slow-cooker size: 3-qt.

11-oz. can mandarin oranges

8½-oz. can sliced peaches in juice, undrained

8-oz. can pineapple tidbits in juice, undrained

1 medium onion, chopped finely

½ cup finely chopped green bell pepper

½ cup finely chopped red bell pepper

1 jalapeño pepper, chopped finely

3 cloves garlic, minced

3 Tbsp. cornstarch

1 tsp. salt

juice of 1 lime

zest of 1 lime, cut in fine strips (not finely grated)

¼ cup chopped cilantro

tortilla chips, for serving

1. Combine fruits, onion, peppers, garlic, cornstarch, and salt in slow cooker.

2. Cover and cook on High for 2 hours, stirring once each hour. Salsa should be thick and steaming, the peppers softened.

3. Add lime juice and zest. Add cilantro. Remove salsa from slow cooker to serving dish. Allow to cool for about 15 minutes before serving with tortilla chips.

Good go-alongs with this recipe:

Delicious on top of a cheese omelet at breakfast.

TIPS

I use my vegetable peeler to take off the skin of the lime, then I chop it into narrow strips with a knife. There are also some zesters that make ribbons of zest instead of finely grated zest. The strips of lime zest look pretty in the salsa.

Peach Chutney

Jan Mast, Lancaster, PA

Makes 32 servings

Prep. Time: 20 minutes ❧ *Cooking Time: 5–8 hours* ❧ *Ideal slow-cooker size: 4-qt.*

2 29-oz. cans (about 6 cups) peaches in sugar-free syrup, diced

1 cup raisins

1 small onion, chopped

1 clove garlic, minced

1 Tbsp. ground mustard seeds

1 tsp. dried red chilies, chopped

2 oz. crystallized ginger, chopped

1 tsp. salt

¾ cup vinegar

½ cup brown sugar

1. Combine all ingredients in slow cooker.

2. Cover. Cook on Low 4–6 hours.

3. Remove lid. Stir chutney. Cook on High, uncovered, an additional 1–2 hours.

Basil Mint Tea

Nancy T. Dickman, Marblemount, WA

Makes 10 servings

Prep. Time: 10 minutes & Cooking Time: 2 hours & Ideal slow-cooker size: 3-qt.

20 fresh basil leaves, or 3 Tbsp. dried

20 fresh spearmint or peppermint
leaves, or 3 Tbsp. dried

10 cups water

¼ cup sugar

1. Place herbs in slow cooker. If using fresh herbs, mash gently with a spoon. If using dried herbs, put in tea-ball infusers or cheesecloth bag.

2. Add water and sugar.

3. Cover and cook on Low for 2 hours, until fragrant and steaming. Serve hot, or chill completely and serve cold.

TIP
You may mix some lemonade and lemon slices in the chilled tea.

Green Grape Ginger Tea

Evelyn Page, Gillette, WY

Makes 8 cups

Prep. Time: 5–15 minutes ❧ *Cooking Time: 2 hours* ❧ *Ideal slow-cooker size: 3-qt.*

4 cups boiling water

15 single green tea bags

4 cups white grape juice

1 Tbsp. honey

1 Tbsp. minced fresh gingerroot

1. Place boiling water and tea bags in slow cooker. Cover and let stand 10 minutes. Discard tea bags.

2. Stir in juice, honey, and gingerroot.

3. Cover. Cook on Low 2 hours, or until heated through.

4. Strain if you wish before pouring into individual cups.

Chicken & Turkey Main Dishes

Chili Barbecue Chicken Wings

Rosemarie Fitzgerald, Gibsonia, PA

Makes 10 full-sized servings

Prep. Time: 5 minutes   ♣   Cooking Time: 2–8 hours   ♣   Ideal slow-cooker size: 5-qt.

5 lbs. chicken wings, tips cut off
12-oz. bottle chili sauce
⅓ cup lemon juice
1 Tbsp. Worcestershire sauce
2 Tbsp. molasses
1 tsp. salt
2 tsp. chili powder
⅓ tsp. hot pepper sauce
dash garlic powder

1. Place wings in cooker.

2. Combine remaining ingredients and pour over chicken.

3. Cover. Cook on Low 6–8 hours, or on High 2–3 hours.

NOTE

These wings are also a great appetizer, yielding about 15 appetizer-sized servings. Take any leftover chicken off the bone and combine with leftover sauce. Serve over cooked pasta for a second meal.

Heavenly Barbecued Chicken Wings

Tracy Supcoe, Barclay, MD

Makes 8 full-sized servings

Prep. Time: 20 minutes & Cooking Time: 5–6 hours & Ideal slow-cooker size: 5-qt.

4 lbs. chicken wings
2 large onions, chopped
2 6-oz. cans tomato paste
2 large cloves garlic, minced
¼ cup Worcestershire sauce
¼ cup cider vinegar
½ cup brown sugar
½ cup sweet pickle relish
½ cup red, or white, wine
2 tsp. salt
2 tsp. dry mustard

1. Cut off wing tips. Cut wings at joint. Place in slow cooker.

2. Combine remaining ingredients. Add to slow cooker. Stir.

3. Cover. Cook on Low 5–6 hours.

Mouth-Watering Barbecued Chicken Wings

Mary L. Casey, Scranton, PA

Makes 8–12 full-sized servings

Prep. Time: 10 minutes ⚗ Cooking Time: 4–6 hours ⚗ Ideal slow-cooker size: 4- to 5-qt.

3–6 lbs. chicken wings
1–3 Tbsp. oil
¾–1 cup vinegar
½ cup ketchup
2 Tbsp. sugar
2 Tbsp. Worcestershire sauce
3 cloves garlic, minced
1 Tbsp. dry mustard
1 tsp. paprika
½–1 tsp. salt
⅛ tsp. pepper

1. Brown wings in oil in skillet, or brush wings with oil and broil, watching carefully so they do not burn.

2. Combine remaining ingredients in slow cooker. Add wings. Stir gently so that they are all well covered with sauce.

3. Cover. Cook on Low 4–6 hours, or until tender.

BBQ Chicken Sandwiches

Sarah Herr, Goshen, IN

Makes 8 servings

Prep. Time: 15 minutes ❧ *Cooking Time: 4 hours* ❧ *Ideal slow-cooker size: 5-qt.*

3 lbs. boneless, skinless chicken thighs

1 onion, chopped

½ cup brown sugar

½ cup apple cider vinegar

½ cup ketchup

1 tsp. dry mustard

1 tsp. cumin

1 Tbsp. chili powder

½ tsp. black pepper

8 hamburger buns

1. Grease interior of slow-cooker crock.

2. Place chicken into crock. If you need to make a second layer, stagger the pieces so they don't directly overlap each other.

3. Mix other ingredients together well in a bowl.

4. Spoon over thighs. Make sure the ones on the bottom layer get covered too.

5. Cover. Cook on Low 4 hours, or until instant-read meat thermometer registers 160 degrees when stuck in center of thighs.

6. Lift cooked chicken out of crock and shred with two forks.

7. Stir shredded meat back into sauce in crock.

8. Serve on hamburger buns.

Jazzed-Up Barbecue Pulled Chicken

Hope Comerford, Clinton Township, MI

Makes 6–8 servings

Prep. Time: 5 minutes & Cooking Time: 6–7 hours & Ideal slow-cooker size: 4-qt.

2 lbs. boneless skinless chicken breasts

1 cup ketchup

¼ cup molasses

2 Tbsp. apple cider vinegar

2 Tbsp. Worcestershire sauce

1 clove garlic, minced

2 tsp. dry mustard

2 Tbsp. orange juice

1 tsp. orange zest

1. Place chicken in crock.

2. In a bowl, mix together the ketchup, molasses, apple cider vinegar, Worcestershire sauce, minced garlic, mustard powder, orange juice, and orange zest. Pour over the chicken.

3. Cover and cook on Low for 6–7 hours.

4. Remove the chicken and shred between two forks, then stir back through the sauce in the crock.

Serving suggestion:

Serve on buns with your favorite toppings.

Tropical Barbecue Pulled Chicken

Hope Comerford, Clinton Township, MI

Makes 6–8 servings

Prep. Time: 5 minutes   &   Cooking Time: 6–7 hours   &   Ideal slow-cooker size: 4-qt.

3 lbs. boneless skinless chicken

29-oz. can tomato sauce

20-oz. can unsweetened crushed pineapple, undrained

2 Tbsp. brown sugar

3 Tbsp. apple cider vinegar

2 Tbsp. dry mustard

1 Tbsp. dried minced onion

2 tsp. Worcestershire sauce

¼ tsp. garlic powder

⅛ tsp. pepper

1. Place the chicken in the crock.

2. In a bowl, mix together the remaining ingredients, then pour over the chicken.

3. Cover and cook on Low for 6–7 hours.

4. Remove the chicken and shred between two forks. Place the chicken back in the crock and stir through the sauce.

Serving suggestion:

Serve on buns with your favorite toppings.

Slow Cooker Burritos

Hope Comerford, Clinton Township, MI

Makes 8 servings

Prep. Time: 10 minutes ♣ Cooking Time: 5 hours ♣ Ideal slow-cooker size: 3-qt.

1½ lbs. boneless skinless chicken breasts

15-oz. can pinto beans, drained and rinsed

2 cups salsa

1 cup chicken stock

1 small onion, chopped

4-oz. can diced green chilies

1 cup frozen corn

2 Tbsp. chili powder

1 tsp. cumin

1½ tsp. salt

½ cup brown rice

8 round flour tortillas

1. Place the chicken in the crock.

2. In a bowl, mix together the pinto beans, salsa, chicken stock, onion, green chilies, corn, chili powder, cumin, and salt. Pour this over the chicken.

3. Cover and cook on Low for 3 hours. Stir in the rice.

4. Cover again and cook on Low for an additional 2 hours.

5. Remove and shred the chicken between two forks. Stir it back through the contents of the crock.

6. Fill each tortilla with the burrito filling and wrap them up.

Pineapple Jalapeño Chicken

Hope Comerford, Clinton Township, MI

Makes about 6 kabobs

Prep. Time: 20 minutes   Cooking Time: 5 hours   Broil Time: 3–5 minutes   Ideal slow-cooker size: 6-qt.

2 cups frozen pineapple chunks

12-oz. jar mild jalapeño jelly

¼ cup pineapple juice

½ tsp. salt

⅛ tsp. pepper

1½ lbs. boneless skinless chicken thighs, cut into large bite-sized pieces

1. Let the pineapple sit out for a few minutes, just so you can get through it with the skewers.

2. Meanwhile, soak your skewers in water and cut them to fit your crock if needed.

3. In a bowl, mix together the jalapeño jelly, pineapple juice, salt, and pepper. Set aside.

4. Skewer the pineapple and chicken, alternating between the two. Place them in the crock.

5. Pour all but 2–3 Tbsp. of the jelly mixture over the skewers in the crock.

6. Cover and cook on Low for 5 hours.

7. Remove the skewers and place them on a foil-lined baking sheet. Brush them with the remaining sauce and place them under the broiler for 3–5 minutes.

Italian Chicken Fajita Wraps

Phyllis Good, Lancaster, PA

Makes 4–6 servings

Prep. Time: 20 minutes   ⚬   Cooking Time: 2–4 hours
Chilling Time: 4–8 hours or overnight   ⚬   Ideal slow-cooker size: 3-qt.

I lb. boneless, skinless chicken breasts
2 cloves garlic, sliced thinly
2 Tbsp. dried oregano
I Tbsp. dried parsley
I tsp. dried basil
½ tsp. dried thyme
¼ tsp. celery seed
I Tbsp. sugar
½ tsp. salt
I tsp. freshly ground pepper
8-oz. bottle Italian salad dressing
I cup salsa
I green bell pepper, sliced in ribs
I red bell pepper, sliced in ribs
I medium onion, sliced in rings
10 10-inch-flour tortillas

Toppings (choose all or some):
freshly grated Parmesan cheese
fresh mozzarella slices
hot sauce, or pickled Italian hot peppers
chopped olives
lemon wedges
shredded lettuce
chopped tomatoes
chopped fresh basil

1. Cut chicken into thin strips. Place in large mixing bowl.

2. Add garlic, herbs, sugar, salt, pepper, salad dressing, and salsa. Mix well. Cover and marinate 4–8 hours or overnight in the fridge.

3. Pour chicken and marinade into slow cooker. Cook on Low for 2–4 hours, until chicken is white through the middle and tender.

4. Spoon the chicken with its sauce into an ovenproof serving dish or rimmed baking sheet. Add the vegetables. Slide it under the broiler for a few minutes until browned spots appear on the chicken and vegetables.

5. Serve with tortillas and toppings and lots of napkins.

Basil Chicken

Phyllis Good, Lancaster, PA

Makes 4–6 servings

Prep. Time: 15 minutes ⚥ *Cooking Time: 4¼–4½ hours* ⚥ *Ideal slow-cooker size: 4-qt.*

2 pounds boneless, skinless chicken thighs

14½-oz. can diced tomatoes with juice

14½-oz can garbanzo beans, drained and rinsed

2 Tbsp. capers with their brine

2 cloves garlic, sliced thinly

⅛ tsp. freshly ground black pepper

1 tsp. dried basil

8 oz. crumbled feta cheese

¼ cup tightly packed basil leaves, chopped

1. Place chicken in slow cooker. Pour tomatoes, garbanzos, and capers on top.

2. Sprinkle with garlic slices, pepper, and dried basil.

3. Cover and cook on Low 4 hours.

4. Sprinkle with feta. Cook on Low for 15–30 more minutes, or until chicken is done.

5. Sprinkle with fresh basil and serve. Great served with pasta or crusty bread to handle the sauce.

Herbed Chicken

Phyllis Good, Lancaster, PA

Makes 4–6 servings

Prep. Time: 15 minutes   Cooking Time: 4–6 hours   Ideal slow-cooker size: 6-qt.

5-lb. roasting chicken
1 onion, quartered
2 cloves garlic, 1 sliced, 1 whole
1 Tbsp. fresh parsley, or 1 tsp. dried
1 Tbsp. fresh sage, or 1 tsp. dried
1 Tbsp. fresh rosemary, or 1 tsp. dried
1 Tbsp. fresh thyme, or 1 tsp. dried
1 Tbsp. butter, softened
paprika to taste
salt to taste
pepper to taste

1. Grease crock of slow cooker. Clean and wash the chicken. Pat dry.

2. Put the quartered onion and sliced garlic into the bird's cavity. Stuff in the parsley, sage, rosemary, and thyme too.

3. Rub the outside of the chicken with the whole garlic clove, and then toss it into the cavity.

4. Rub the outside of the chicken with softened butter. Sprinkle with paprika, salt, and pepper.

5. Place chicken into the greased slow cooker.

6. Cover. Cook on Low 4–6 hours, or until the meat is tender, the drumsticks move freely, and the juices run clear.

7. Lift the chicken out of the cooker onto a platter. Cover with foil to keep warm. Let it stand for 15 minutes before cutting it up.

8. Thicken the chicken stock to make gravy. Or use the broth to make rice.

Herby Chicken with Pesto

Phyllis Good, Lancaster, PA

Makes 6–8 servings

Prep. Time: 20 minutes   ❧   *Cooking Time: 4–6 hours*   ❧   *Ideal slow-cooker size: 6-qt.*

Pesto ingredients:

2 cups fresh basil, or 2 Tbsp. dried basil

½ cup olive oil

2 Tbsp. pine nuts

2 cloves garlic, crushed

1 tsp. salt

½ cup Parmesan cheese, freshly grated

2 Tbsp. Romano cheese, grated

3 Tbsp. butter, softened

Chicken ingredients:

6 medium onions, coarsely chopped

2 Tbsp. olive oil

2 28-oz. cans plum tomatoes, undrained

1 Tbsp. fresh thyme, or 1 tsp. dried thyme

1 Tbsp. fresh basil, or 1 tsp. dried basil

1 Tbsp. fresh tarragon, or 1 tsp. dried tarragon

1 Tbsp. fresh rosemary, or 1 tsp. fresh rosemary

4 cloves garlic, minced

2 cups chicken broth

4 cups dry white wine

2–3 lbs. chicken thighs, bone in, skin removed

1½–2 lbs. small new potatoes, unpeeled

2 loaves French bread, sliced and warmed

1. Make the pesto first. Blend all its ingredients together, except the cheeses and softened butter, in a blender or food processor. Pour the mixture into a bowl and then stir in the cheeses and butter.

2. Put the onions, olive oil, tomatoes with their juice, all the herbs, the garlic, chicken broth, wine, and half the pesto into your slow cooker. Mix everything together well.

3. Nestle the chicken thighs into the tomatoey broth, submerging them as much as you can.

4. Add the potatoes, pushing them down into the broth too.

5. Cover. Cook on Low 4–6 hours, or until the potatoes are soft when you jag them with a fork and the chicken is tender.

6. Serve in deep soup plates with plenty of hot French bread to mop up the juices. Serve the remaining pesto at the table.

Sunny Chicken

Phyllis Good, Lancaster, PA

Makes 4–5 servings

Prep. Time: 20–30 minutes   ⚶   *Cooking Time: 4–6 hours*   ⚶   *Ideal slow-cooker size: 6-qt.*

I large onion, sliced into thin rings, *divided*

3 sweet, juicy oranges, each cut into thin slices, *divided*

3 lemons, thinly sliced, *divided*

3 limes, thinly sliced, *divided*

9 fresh rosemary sprigs, *divided*

2 Tbsp. minced garlic, *divided*

5-lb. chicken

salt and pepper to taste

1. Layer ⅓ of the onion slices, 1 sliced orange, 1 sliced lemon, and 1 sliced lime into your slow cooker. Top with 3 rosemary sprigs and ⅓ of the minced garlic.

2. Stuff chicken with half the remaining onion slices, 1 sliced orange, 1 sliced lemon, and 1 sliced lime, half the remaining garlic, and 3 rosemary sprigs. Place the stuffed chicken—upside down—in your slow cooker. (That helps to keep the breast meat from drying out.)

3. Sprinkle with plenty of salt and pepper. Spread the rest of the onion, orange, lemon, and lime slices, and the remaining garlic and rosemary sprigs, around the chicken and on top of it.

4. Cover. Cook on Low 4–6 hours, or until meat is tender but not dry.

5. Remove chicken from cooker and place right-side up on rimmed baking sheet. Place under broiler until top is nicely browned, only a minute or so, watching closely.

6. Cover chicken with foil for 15 minutes. Then carve, put the pieces on a platter, and spoon the citrus and onion slices over top before serving.

Sweet Islands Chicken

Cynthia Morris, Grottoes, VA

Makes 6 servings

Prep. Time: 15–20 minutes ⚘ *Cooking Time: 3–4 hours* ⚘ *Ideal slow-cooker size: 4-qt.*

I cup pineapple juice

½ cup brown sugar

⅓ cup soy sauce

2 lbs. boneless, skinless chicken thighs, cut in 1-inch chunks

I Tbsp., plus I tsp., cornstarch

1. Grease interior of slow-cooker crock.

2. Mix pineapple juice, brown sugar, and soy sauce together in crock until well combined.

3. Stir in chicken chunks.

4. Cover. Cook on Low 3–4 hours, or until meat is cooked in center, but not dry.

5. When done cooking, spoon 1 Tbsp. and 1 tsp. sauce out of cooker and allow to cool in a small bowl.

6. Stir cornstarch into cooled sauce until smooth.

7. Stir cornstarch-sauce mix back into hot sauce remaining in crock. Continue stirring until sauce thickens.

Serving suggestion:

Serve chicken and sauce over cooked rice or noodles.

Variations:

From the tester: Add ½ cup diced onion and ½ tsp. minced fresh ginger to Step 2.
—Anita Troyer

Memories of Tucson Chicken

Joanna Harrison, Lafayette, CO

Makes 6 servings

Prep. Time: 20 minutes ♣ Cooking Time: 4 hours ♣ Ideal slow-cooker size: 6-qt.

1 medium onion, chopped coarsely

3 cloves garlic, minced

2–3 green chilies, chopped, or 4-oz. can chopped green chilies

1 cup chopped tomatoes

2 cups corn, fresh, frozen, or canned

2 tsp. dried oregano

1 tsp. ground cumin

1 tsp. dried basil

2 cups chicken broth

6 boneless, skinless chicken thighs

1 green bell pepper, chopped

1–2 zucchini, chopped

¼–½ cup cilantro leaves

1. Grease interior of slow-cooker crock.

2. Place onion, garlic, chilies, tomatoes, corn, oregano, cumin, basil, and broth in slow cooker. Stir until well mixed.

3. Place chicken in broth, submerging until covered, or nearly so.

4. Cover. Cook on Low 3 hours.

5. Lift out thighs and keep covered on platter.

6. Stir in bell pepper and zucchini.

7. Return chicken to cooker, again pushing the pieces down into the liquid.

8. Cover and continue cooking 1 more hour on Low, or until an instant-read meat thermometer registers 160–165°F when stuck in the thighs.

9. Place the chicken on a platter. Spoon vegetables and broth over top. Scatter cilantro leaves over all and serve.

Sweet and Sour Chicken

Janette Fox, Honey Brook, PA

Makes 6–8 servings

Prep. Time: 15 minutes ❧ Cooking Time: 4 hours ❧ Ideal slow-cooker size: 5-qt.

3 lbs. boneless, skinless chicken thighs
½ cup chopped onions
½ green pepper, chopped
15-oz. can pineapple chunks in juice
¾ cup ketchup
¼ cup brown sugar, packed
2 Tbsp. apple cider vinegar
2 tsp. soy sauce
½ tsp. garlic salt
½ tsp. salt
¼ tsp. black pepper
cooked rice

1. Grease interior of slow-cooker crock.

2. Put chicken in crock. If you need to add a second layer, stagger the pieces so they don't directly overlap each other.

3. Scatter onions and green pepper over top.

4. In a mixing bowl, combine pineapple chunks and juice, ketchup, brown sugar, vinegar, soy sauce, garlic salt, salt, and black pepper.

5. Spoon over chicken, onions, and green pepper.

6. Cover. Cook on Low 4 hours, or until instant-read meat thermometer registers 165°F when stuck into center of thighs.

7. Serve over cooked rice.

Chicken and Biscuits

Hope Comerford, Clinton Township, MI

Makes 4–6 servings

Prep. Time: 5 minutes ⚖ *Cooking Time: 6 hours* ⚖ *Ideal slow-cooker size: 3-qt.*

2 lbs. boneless skinless chicken breasts

10½-oz. can condensed cream of chicken soup

10½-oz. can condensed cream of potato soup

¾ cup milk

½ tsp. salt

⅛ tsp. pepper

2 tsp. garlic powder

2 tsp. onion powder

1 cup frozen mixed vegetables

6 refrigerator biscuits, cooked according to the package directions

1. Place the boneless skinless chicken in the crock.

2. In a bowl, mix together the cream of chicken soup, cream of potato soup, milk, salt, pepper, garlic powder, onion powder, and frozen mixed vegetables. Pour this over the chicken.

3. Cover and cook on Low for 6 hours.

4. Shred the chicken between two forks and stir back through the contents of the crock.

5. Serve the chicken mixture over the biscuits to serve.

Barbecued Turkey Cutlets

Phyllis Good, Lancaster, PA

Makes 6–8 servings

Prep. Time: 10 minutes ♣ Cooking Time: 4 hours ♣ Ideal slow-cooker size: 4- or 5-qt.

6–8 (1½–2 lbs.) turkey cutlets
¼ cup molasses
¼ cup apple cider vinegar
½ cup ketchup
3 Tbsp. Worcestershire sauce
1 tsp. garlic salt
3 Tbsp. chopped onion
2 Tbsp. brown sugar
¼–½ tsp. pepper

1. Place turkey cutlets in slow cooker.

2. Combine remaining ingredients in a bowl. Pour over turkey.

3. Cover. Cook on Low 4 hours.

Serving suggestion:
Serve over white or brown rice.

Glazed Barbecue Turkey Meatloaf

Hope Comerford, Clinton Township, MI

Makes 6–8 servings

Prep. Time: 15–20 minutes & Cooking Time: 4–5 hours & Ideal slow-cooker size: 5-qt. oval

2 lbs. ground turkey

1 large egg

1¼ cups gluten-free or regular panko bread crumbs

1 Tbsp. garlic powder

1 Tbsp. onion powder

3 tsp. dried minced onion

1 tsp. Italian seasoning

6 dashes Worcestershire sauce

¼ cup barbecue sauce

Glaze:

3 Tbsp. brown sugar

¼ cup barbecue sauce

1 tsp. dry mustard

1. Spray crock with nonstick spray.

2. Make a tinfoil sling for your slow cooker so you can lift the cooked meatloaf out easily. Begin by folding a strip of foil accordion-fashion so that it's about 1½–2 inches wide, and long enough to fit from the top edge of the crock, down inside and up the other side, plus a 2-inch overhang on each side of the cooker. Make a second strip exactly like the first.

3. Place the one strip in the crock, running from end to end. Place the second strip in the crock, running from side to side. The 2 strips should form a cross in the bottom of the crock.

4. In a bowl, mix together all of the meatloaf ingredients, then shape it into a loaf. Place it in the crock, centering it where the foil handles cross.

5. Cover and cook on Low 4–5 hours.

6. Remove the meatloaf from the crock using the handles and place on a baking sheet.

7. Mix the glaze ingredients together. Spoon this over the top of the meatloaf.

8. Place the meatloaf in the oven under the broiler for 2–4 minutes, so that the glaze thickens and browns, but be careful not to let it burn.

9. Let it stand for 10 minutes, then slice and serve.

Pork Main Dishes

Easiest Ever BBQ Country Ribs

Hope Comerford, Clinton Township, MI

Makes 4–6 servings

Prep. Time: 5 minutes & Cooking Time: 8–10 hours & Ideal slow-cooker size: 6-qt.

4 lbs. boneless country-style ribs

salt and pepper to taste

18-oz. bottle of your favorite barbecue sauce

1. Place your country ribs into your crock and sprinkle them with salt and pepper on both sides.

2. Pour half the bottle of barbecue sauce on one side of the ribs. Flip them over and poor the other half of the sauce on the other side of your ribs. Spread it around.

3. Cover and cook on Low for 8–10 hours.

Saucy Spareribs

Phyllis Good, Lancaster, PA

Makes 4 servings

Prep. Time: 15 minutes   ❧   *Cooking Time: 4–6 hours*   ❧   *Ideal slow-cooker size: 6-qt.*

3–4 lbs. country-style pork spareribs, cut into serving-sized pieces

¾ cup ketchup

1–2 Tbsp. sriracha sauce, depending how much heat you like, *optional*

3 Tbsp. packed brown sugar

¼ cup honey

¼ cup lemon juice

2 Tbsp. soy sauce

¾ tsp. ground ginger

¼ tsp. chili powder

¼ tsp. dry mustard

¼ tsp. garlic powder

¼ tsp. black pepper (coarsely ground is best)

1. Place cut-up ribs into slow cooker.

2. Mix all remaining ingredients together in a bowl until well combined.

3. Pour over ribs.

4. Cover. Cook on Low 4–6 hours, or until the meat begins to fall off the bones.

Variation:

Double the amount of sauce if you like a lot to eat with the ribs, or if you're serving them with pasta, rice, or potatoes and want to spoon sauce over top.

Barbecued Pork Ribs

Michele Ruvola, Selden, NY

Makes 8 servings

Prep. Time: 5 minutes ⚸ *Cooking Time: 9–10 hours* ⚸ *Ideal slow-cooker size: 4-qt.*

2 Tbsp. dried minced onion

1 tsp. crushed red pepper

½ tsp. ground cinnamon

½ tsp. garlic powder

3 lbs. pork loin back ribs, cut into serving-sized pieces

1 medium onion, sliced

½ cup water

1½ cups barbecue sauce

1. Combine onion, red pepper, cinnamon, and garlic powder. Rub mixture into ribs. Layer ribs and onion in slow cooker. Pour water around ribs.

2. Cover. Cook on Low 8–9 hours.

3. Remove ribs from slow cooker. Drain and discard liquid. Pour barbecue sauce in bowl and dip ribs in sauce. Return ribs to slow cooker. Pour remaining sauce over ribs.

4. Cover. Cook on Low 1 hour.

Tender and Tangy Ribs

Betty Moore, Plano, IL
Renee Shirk, Mount Joy, PA

Makes 2–3 servings

Prep. Time: 10 minutes ⚘ *Cooking Time: 4–6 hours* ⚘ *Ideal slow-cooker size: 2- to 3-qt.*

¾–1 cup vinegar
½ cup ketchup
2 Tbsp. sugar
2 Tbsp. Worcestershire sauce
1 clove garlic, minced
1 tsp. dry mustard
1 tsp. paprika
½ tsp. salt
⅛ tsp. pepper
2 lbs. pork spareribs
1 Tbsp. oil

1. Combine all ingredients except spareribs and oil in slow cooker.

2. Brown ribs in oil in skillet. Transfer to slow cooker.

3. Cover. Cook on Low 4–6 hours.

Awfully Easy Barbecued Ribs

Sara Harter Fredette, Williamsburg, MA
Colleen Konetzni, Rio Rancho, NM
Mary Mitchell, Battle Creek, MI
Audrey Romonosky, Austin, TX
Iva Schmidt, Fergus Falls, MN
Susan Tjon, Austin, TX

Makes 4–6 servings

Prep. Time: 10 minutes ☙ Cooking Time: 6 hours ☙ Ideal slow-cooker size: 4- to 5-qt.

3–4-lbs. baby back, or country-style, spareribs

½ tsp. salt, *optional*

½ tsp. pepper, *optional*

2 onions, sliced

16–24-oz. bottle barbecue sauce (depending upon how saucy you like your chops)

1. Brown ribs under broiler. Slice into serving-sized pieces, season, and place in slow cooker.

2. Add onions and barbecue sauce.

3. Cover. Cook on Low 6 hours.

Serving suggestion:

These are good served with baked beans and corn on the cob.

Variation:

Instead of broiling the ribs, place them in slow cooker with other ingredients and cook on High 1 hour. Turn to Low and cook 8 more hours.

Tomato-Glazed Pork with Grilled Corn Salsa

Janet Melvin, Cincinnati, OH

Makes 6–8 servings

Prep. Time: 45 minutes ⚜ Cooking Time: 3–4 hours ⚜ Ideal slow-cooker size: 5-qt.

Tomato Glaze:

2 Tbsp. dry mustard

I Tbsp. ground ginger

I Tbsp. ground fennel

I Tbsp. minced garlic

¼ cup mayonnaise

I cup ketchup

¼ cup honey

I Tbsp. Worcestershire sauce

¼ cup grated fresh horseradish

3 Tbsp. white wine mustard

2 Tbsp. minced capers

I Tbsp. Tabasco sauce

2-lb. boneless pork loin roast, short and wide in shape

Salsa:

3 ears sweet corn, husked and silked, or 4 cups frozen or canned corn

½ cup olive oil

¼ cup chopped sun-dried tomatoes

I clove garlic, minced

½ cup wild mushrooms, sliced

2 Tbsp. chopped fresh cilantro

2 Tbsp. fresh lime juice

I chipotle pepper in adobo sauce, finely chopped

½ tsp. salt

1. Grease interior of slow-cooker crock.

2. Prepare glaze by mixing together dry mustard, ginger, fennel, garlic, and mayonnaise.

3. When well blended, stir in remaining glaze ingredients.

4. Place pork in slow cooker, fat side up. Cover with glaze.

5. Cover. Cook on Low 3–4 hours, or until instant-read meat thermometer registers 140°F when stuck into center of roast.

6. While roast is cooking, brush ears of corn with olive oil. Wrap in foil.

7. Bake at 350°F for 15 minutes. Unwrap and grill or broil until evenly browned.

8. Cool. Cut kernels from cob.

9. Combine corn with rest of salsa ingredients.

10. Cover and refrigerate until ready to use.

11. When pork is finished cooking, remove from cooker to cutting board. Cover with foil and let stand for 10 minutes.

12. Slice and serve on top of grilled corn salsa.

Pulled Pork

Janet Batdorf, Harrisburg, PA

Makes 10 servings

Prep. Time: 20 minutes & Cooking Time: 9 hours
Chilling Time for broth: 4–5 hours & Ideal slow-cooker size: 5-qt.

3-lb. pork roast

Sauce:
1 cup ketchup
1 cup pork broth
2 Tbsp. Worcestershire sauce
2 Tbsp. vinegar
dash pepper
¾ tsp. salt
2 Tbsp. prepared mustard
1 large onion, chopped

1. Place pork in slow cooker.

2. Cover with water.

3. Cover. Cook overnight, or for approximately 8 hours, on Low.

4. Turn off slow cooker.

5. Remove pork and set aside.

6. Refrigerate broth.

7. Skim off fat when cold.

8. Combine sauce ingredients in slow cooker.

9. Shred pork with two forks.

10. Add shredded pork to sauce.

11. Turn slow cooker on Low. Heat pork in sauce for about one hour, or until ingredients are hot and bubbly.

Serving suggestion:

Serve in buns, or over mashed potatoes, or rice, or pasta.

Slow-Cooked Barbecue Pork

Sharon Wantland, Menomonee Falls, WI

Makes 8 servings

Prep. Time: 15–20 minutes ⚬ *Cooking Time: 5–6 hours* ⚬ *Ideal slow-cooker size: 4-qt.*

3–4-lb. boneless pork loin roast
1½ tsp. seasoned salt
1 tsp. garlic powder
1 cup barbecue sauce
1 cup cola, regular or diet

1. Cut roast in half. Place both halves in slow cooker.

2. Sprinkle with seasoned salt and garlic powder.

3. Cover. Cook 4 hours on Low.

4. Remove meat.

5. Skim fat from broth remaining in slow cooker.

6. Shred pork using two forks.

7. Return shredded pork to slow cooker.

8. Combine barbecue sauce and cola in a small bowl.

9. Pour over meat.

10. Cover. Cook on High 1–2 hours, or until heated through and bubbly.

Serving suggestion:

Serve on buns.

Smoked Barbecue Pork Sandwiches

Hope Comerford, Clinton Township, MI

Makes 8 servings

Prep. Time: 15–20 minutes ⚬ *Cooking Time: 9 hours* ⚬ *Ideal slow-cooker size: 4-qt.*

4–5-lb. beef brisket
⅛ tsp. celery salt
¼ tsp. garlic salt
¼ tsp. onion salt
¼ tsp. salt
3 Tbsp. liquid smoke
1½ cups barbecue sauce

1. Place brisket in slow cooker.

2. Sprinkle with celery salt, garlic salt, onion salt, and salt.

3. Pour liquid smoke over brisket. Cover. Refrigerate for 8 hours.

4. Cook on Low 8–10 hours, or until tender. During last hour, pour barbecue sauce over brisket.

Barbecued Pork Steaks

Marcia S. Myer, Manheim, PA

Makes 4 servings

Prep. Time: 15–20 minutes ❧ *Cooking Time: 8 hours* ❧ *Ideal slow-cooker size: 5-qt.*

4 pork shoulder steaks, cut ½-inch thick

1 Tbsp. oil

1 large onion, sliced

1 large green pepper, sliced

2 tomatoes, sliced

1 Tbsp. instant tapioca

½ cup barbecue sauce

¼ cup red wine

½ tsp. cumin

1. Brown steaks in hot oil in skillet.

2. In slow cooker, arrange slices of onion, green pepper, and tomato.

3. Sprinkle tapioca over vegetables.

4. Place browned pork steaks on top of vegetables.

5. In bowl combine barbecue sauce, wine, and cumin.

6. Pour over meat.

7. Cover. Cook 8 hours on Low.

Terrific Tenders

Carol Turner, Mountain City, GA

Makes 8 servings

Prep. Time: 15–20 minutes ♣ Cooking Time: 3–4 hours
Marinating Time: 8 hours or overnight ♣ Ideal slow-cooker size: oval 6- or 7-qt.

3–4-lb. boneless pork loin roast, wide and short (not skinny and long)

7–9 cloves garlic, halved or quartered lengthwise

salt to taste

pepper to taste

2–2½ cups opal basil, raspberry, or blackberry vinegar, or your favorite fruity vinegar

1 Tbsp. butter

2 Tbsp. oil

1 Tbsp. chopped shallots

1½ tsp. dried tarragon

1½ tsp. Dijon mustard

fresh parsley sprigs

1. Pierce roast with knife about ½-inch deep at 2-inch intervals. Insert piece of garlic in each slit.

2. Place roast in covered container to marinate. Sprinkle all over with salt and pepper.

3. Pour in enough vinegar to come at least halfway up sides of roast.

4. Cover. Refrigerate for 8 hours or overnight. Turn meat over a couple of times in marinade.

5. Grease interior of slow-cooker crock.

6. Remove meat from marinade. If you have time, brown in butter and oil on all sides in large skillet. Using strong tongs or two metal spatulas, lift out of skillet and place in crock. If you don't have time, place roast straight from marinade into crock. (Reserve marinade.)

7. Cover cooker. Cook on Low 3–4 hours, or until instant-read meat thermometer registers 145°F when stuck in center of roast.

8. Near end of roast's cooking time, melt butter in skillet. Sauté shallots until softened. Stir in tarragon and mustard. Mix well.

9. Stir 1½–2 cups reserved marinade into mixture in skillet. Reduce heat and cook until slightly thickened and creamy. Set aside, but keep warm until serving time.

10. Remove roast from cooker to cutting board. Cover and keep warm. Let stand 10 minutes. Then slice.

11. Place slices in deep platter. Cover with warm sauce. Garnish with parsley sprigs and serve.

Chops and Beans

Mary L. Casey, Scranton, PA

Makes 4–6 servings

Prep. Time: 15–20 minutes & *Cooking Time: 4–6 hours* & *Ideal slow-cooker size: 4-qt.*

2 1-lb. cans pork and beans

½ cup ketchup

2 slices bacon, browned and crumbled

½ cup chopped onions, sautéed

1 Tbsp. Worcestershire sauce

¼ cup firmly packed brown sugar

4–6 pork chops

2 tsp. prepared mustard

1 Tbsp. brown sugar

¼ cup ketchup

1 lemon, sliced

1. Combine beans, ½ cup ketchup, bacon, onions, Worcestershire sauce, and ¼ cup brown sugar in slow cooker.

2. Brown chops in skillet. In separate bowl, mix together 2 tsp. mustard, 1 Tbsp. brown sugar, and ¼ cup ketchup. Brush each chop with sauce, then carefully stack into cooker, placing a slice of lemon on each chop. Submerge in bean/bacon mixture.

3. Cover. Cook on Low 4–6 hours.

Carnitas

Hope Comerford, Clinton Township, MI

Makes 6–8 servings

Prep. Time: 15 minutes ⚮ *Cooking Time: 8–10 hours* ⚮ *Ideal slow-cooker size: 5-qt.*

Rub:

3 tsp. garlic powder

3 tsp. onion powder

3 tsp. cumin

2 tsp. salt

1½ tsp. chili powder

1 tsp. cinnamon

3–5 lb. pork shoulder roast

2 bay leaves

2 cups chicken broth

taco shells

Suggested garnishes:

avocado slices

lime slices

shredded cheese

fruit salsa

1. Mix rub spices together.

2. Place the pork roast in the crock then rub it all over with the rub.

3. Place the bay leaves around the roast then carefully pour in the chicken broth around the roast, being careful not to wash off the rub.

4. Cover and cook on Low for 8–10 hours.

5. Remove the bay leaves and discard them.

6. Remove the pork roast, shred between two forks, then replace back in the crock and mix with the juices.

7. Serve in taco shells with the suggested garnishes.

Beef Main Dishes

BBQ Beef Kabobs

Hope Comerford, Clinton Township, MI

Makes about 6 kabobs

Prep. Time: 15 minutes ⚮ Cooking Time: 7–8 hours
Broiling Time: 3–5 minutes ⚮ Ideal slow-cooker size: 6–7 qt.

2 lbs. beef sirloin, cut into strips

I large red onion, cut into large bite-sized chunks

3 cups of your favorite barbecue sauce

3 cloves garlic, minced

I tsp. salt

¼ tsp. pepper

1. Soak the skewers in the water and cut them to fit your crock if needed.

2. While the skewers are soaking, in a bowl, mix together the barbecue sauce, garlic, salt, and pepper.

3. Skewer the beef and red onion onto the skewers, alternating between the two. Place them into the crock.

4. Pour all but about 2–3 Tbsp. of the barbecue sauce over the top of the skewers.

5. Cover and cook on Low for 7–8 hours.

6. Remove the skewers from the crock and place them on a foil-lined baking sheet. Brush them with the remaining sauce and place them under the broiler for 3–5 minutes.

Smoky Brisket

Angeline Lang, Greeley, CO

Makes 8–10 servings

Prep. Time: 5 minutes ♣ Cooking Time: 10–12 hours ♣ Ideal slow-cooker size: 4½- to 5-qt.

2 medium onions, sliced
3–4-lb. beef brisket
1 Tbsp. smoke-flavored salt
1 tsp. celery seed
1 Tbsp. mustard seed
½ tsp. pepper
12-oz. bottle chili sauce

1. Arrange onions in bottom of slow cooker.

2. Sprinkle both sides of meat with smoke-flavored salt.

3. Combine celery seed, mustard seed, pepper, and chili sauce. Pour over meat.

4. Cover. Cook on Low 10–12 hours.

Barbecue Brisket

Patricia Howard, Albuquerque, NM

Makes 8–10 servings

Prep. Time: 5 minutes ❧ Marinating Time: 8 hours
Cooking Time: 8–10 hours ❧ Ideal slow-cooker size: 5-qt.

4–5-lb. beef brisket
⅛ tsp. celery salt
¼ tsp. garlic salt
¼ tsp. onion salt
¼ tsp. salt
3 Tbsp. liquid smoke
1½ cups barbecue sauce

1. Place brisket in slow cooker.

2. Sprinkle with celery salt, garlic salt, onion salt, and salt.

3. Pour liquid smoke over brisket. Cover. Refrigerate for 8 hours.

4. Cook on Low 8–10 hours, or until tender. During last hour, pour barbecue sauce over brisket.

Deep, Dark & Delicious Barbecue Sandwiches

Phyllis Good, Lancaster, PA

Makes 14–18 servings

Prep. Time: 20–30 minutes (use a food chopper) ⚜ *Cooking Time: 5–10 hours* ⚜ *Ideal slow-cooker size: 5-qt.*

3 cups chopped celery

1 cup chopped onions

1 cup ketchup

1 cup barbecue sauce

1 cup water

2 Tbsp. vinegar

2 Tbsp. Worcestershire sauce

¼ cup dark brown sugar

1 tsp. salt

½ tsp. pepper

3–4-lb. boneless chuck roast

14–18 hamburger buns

1. Combine all ingredients except roast and buns in slow cooker. When well mixed, put the roast in the cooker. Spoon sauce over top of it.

2. Cover. Cook on High 5–6 hours, or on Low 8–10 hours.

3. Using two forks, pull the meat apart until it's shredded. You can do this in the cooker, or lift it out and do it on a good-sized platter or in a bowl.

4. Stir shredded meat into sauce. Turn the cooker to High if you're ready to eat soon. Or if it will be a while until mealtime, turn the cooker to Low. You're just making sure that the meat and sauce are heated through completely.

5. Serve on buns.

Tangy Barbecue Sandwiches

Lavina Hochstedler, Grand Blanc, MI
Lois M. Martin, Lititz, PA

Makes 14–18 sandwiches

Prep. Time: 10 minutes ⚘ *Cooking Time: 6–7 hours* ⚘ *Ideal slow-cooker size: 5-qt.*

3 cups chopped celery
1 cup chopped onions
2 cups barbecue sauce
2 tsp. Worcestershire sauce
¼ cup brown sugar
1 tsp. chili powder
1 tsp. salt
½ tsp. pepper
½ tsp. garlic powder
3–4-lb. boneless chuck roast

1. Combine all ingredients except roast in slow cooker. When well mixed, add roast.

2. Cover. Cook on High 6–7 hours.

3. Remove roast. Cool and shred meat. Return to sauce. Heat well.

Serving suggestion:

Serve on hamburger buns.

Cuban Steak for Salad

Hope Comerford, Clinton Township, MI

Makes 6–8 servings

Prep. Time: 10 minutes ⚜ *Marinate Time: 2–8 hours* ⚜ *Cooking Time: 6 hours* ⚜ *Ideal slow-cooker size: 3-qt.*

2 lb. skirt steak

2 limes, juiced

1 orange, juiced

¼ cup olive oil

3 cloves garlic, minced

1 tsp. kosher salt

¼ tsp. pepper

¼ tsp. cumin

salad greens

salad dressing of choice

1. Place skirt steak in a ziplock bag.

2. In a small bowl, mix the remaining ingredients. Pour this over the steak in the bag, seal it, and refrigerate it for 2–8 hours.

3. Place the skirt steak with marinade in the crock.

4. Cover and cook on Low for 6 hours.

5. Remove the steak and let it rest on a cutting board for about 5 minutes. Slice into thin strips against the grain.

6. Serve over salad greens with a light dressing.

Fajita Steak

Becky Harder,
Monument, CO

Makes 6 servings

Prep. Time: 10 minutes ⚘ *Cooking Time: 6–8 hours* ⚘ *Ideal slow-cooker size: 4-qt.*

15-oz. can tomatoes with green chilies

¼ cup salsa, your choice of mild,
medium, or hot

8-oz. can tomato sauce

2 lbs. round steak, cut in 2x4-inch strips

1 envelope dry fajita spice mix

1 cup water, *optional*

1. Combine all ingredients—except water—in your slow cooker.

2. Cover and cook on Low 6–8 hours, or until meat is tender but not overcooked.

3. Check meat occasionally to make sure it isn't cooking dry. If it begins to look dry, stir in water, up to 1 cup.

Serving suggestion:

Serve meat with fried onions and green peppers. Offer shredded cheese, avocado chunks, and sour cream as toppings. Let individual eaters wrap any or all of the ingredients in flour tortillas.

Fabulous Fajitas

Phyllis Good, Lancaster, PA

Makes 4 servings

Prep. Time: 15 minutes ♣ Cooking Time: 3½ hours ♣ Ideal slow-cooker size: 4-qt.

1–1 ½ lbs. flank steak, cut across grain in ½-inch-thick strips

2 Tbsp. lemon juice

1 clove garlic, minced

1 ½ tsp. cumin

½ tsp. red pepper flakes

1 tsp. seasoning salt

2 Tbsp. Worcestershire sauce

1 tsp. chili powder

1 green bell pepper, cut in strips

1 yellow onion, sliced

6–8 warmed tortillas, for serving

favorite toppings: sour cream, chopped fresh cilantro, salsa, shredded cheese, etc.

1. Grease interior of slow-cooker crock.

2. Place beef strips in crock.

3. Stir in lemon juice, garlic, cumin, red pepper flakes, seasoning salt, Worcestershire sauce, and chili powder.

4. Cook on Low 2½ hours, or until beef is nearly tender.

5. Stir in pepper and onion.

6. Cover. Cook for another hour on Low or until vegetables are as tender as you like them.

7. Spoon mixture into warm tortillas. Top with favorite toppings.

Salsa Flank Steak Tacos

Sarah Herr, Goshen, IN

Makes 8 servings

Prep. Time: 20 minutes ⚜ Cooking Time: 6–8 hours ⚜ Ideal slow-cooker size: 4-qt.

2 lbs. flank steak

1 green bell pepper, chopped

1 onion, chopped

1 cup salsa (I use peach flavored, which is less tomatoey)

2 Tbsp., or 1 envelope, taco seasoning

1. Grease interior of slow-cooker crock.

2. Place steak in crock.

3. Mix all other ingredients in a bowl. Spoon over meat.

4. Cover. Cook 6–8 hours on Low, or until instant-read meat thermometer registers 140–145°F when stuck in center.

5. Shred meat with two forks, or slice thinly. Mix with vegetables and juice.

6. Serve with tortillas or taco shells. Or drain and include in a taco salad.

Good go-alongs with this recipe:

Serve with beans, lettuce, tomato, cheese, sour cream, black olives, and your other favorite taco toppings.

Beef Roast with Homemade Ginger-Orange Sauce

Beverly Hummel, Fleetwood, PA

Makes 8 servings

Prep. Time: 20 minutes ❧ *Cooking Time: 8½ hours* ❧ *Ideal slow-cooker size: 7-qt.*

3-lb. boneless chuck roast

salt and pepper to taste

Ginger-Orange Sauce:

2 cups soy sauce

½ cup brown sugar

½ cup white sugar

¼ cup minced onion

I Tbsp. ground ginger

I clove garlic, minced

½ cup orange juice

1. Grease interior of slow-cooker crock.

2. Hold roast over crock; salt and pepper it on all sides.

3. Place roast in cooker. Cover. Cook on Low 8 hours, or until an instant-read meat thermometer registers 150–160°F when stuck in center of roast.

4. While roast is cooking, combine all ingredients for Sauce in saucepan. Stir together until well mixed.

5. Simmer 15 minutes, stirring occasionally so it doesn't stick.

6. Using sturdy tongs or two metal spatulas, lift cooked roast into big bowl. Shred with two forks.

7. Drain drippings and broth out of slow cooker. Save for gravy or soup.

8. Return shredded meat to crock. Stir in 1 cup Ginger-Orange Sauce.

9. Cover. Cook on Low 30 minutes, or until heated through.

TIP

We found this sauce while vacationing on the West Coast, but could find nothing like it where we live on the East Coast. My children asked for it often, so I came up with this homemade sauce that's comparable.

Good go-alongs with this recipe:

Mashed potatoes and green bean casserole.

Serving suggestion:

Serve over mashed potatoes or rice. Or serve in sandwiches.

Walking Tacos

Hope Comerford, Clinton Township, MI

Makes 10–16 servings

Prep. Time: 10 minutes ❧ *Cooking Time: 6–7 hours* ❧ *Ideal slow-cooker size: 2–3 qt.*

2 lbs. ground beef

2 tsp. garlic powder

2 tsp. onion powder

I Tbsp. cumin

2 Tbsp. chili powder

I tsp. salt

½ tsp. oregano

½ tsp. red pepper flakes

I small onion, minced

I clove garlic, minced

10–16 individual sized bags of Doritos

suggested toppings:
diced tomatoes, shredded cheese,
diced cucumbers, chopped onion,
shredded lettuce, sour cream, salsa

1. Crumble the ground beef into the crock.

2. In a bowl, mix together all of the spices, onion, and garlic. Pour this over beef then stir it up.

3. Cover and cook for 6–7 hours, breaking it up every once in a while.

4. Remove some of the grease if you wish.

5. To serve, open up the bag of Doritos, crumble the chips in the bag with your hand, add some of the ground beef to the bag, then any additional toppings you desire. Serve each bag with a fork.

Bacon, Spinach, and Parmesan Stuffed Meatloaf

Hope Comerford, Clinton Township, MI

Makes 4–6 servings

Prep. Time: 25 minutes & Cooking Time: 6–7 hours & Ideal slow-cooker size: 4-qt.

2 lbs. lean ground beef

¾ cup cooked quinoa

1 Tbsp. dry minced onion

1½ tsp. garlic powder

1½ tsp. onion powder

1 tsp. Italian seasoning

1 egg

6 slices bacon

2 cups fresh spinach leaves

1 cup shredded Parmesan cheese

1. In a bowl, mix together the ground beef, quinoa, minced onion, garlic powder, onion powder, Italian seasoning, and egg. Form into a loaf.

2. Place a piece of wax paper on your counter about 2 ft. long. Place the loaf on the wax paper and form it into a ¼-½–inch-thick rectangle.

3. Leaving about an inch on all sides, layer on the bacon, spinach leaves, and parmesan cheese.

4. To roll up: Gently pull up on end of the wax paper so that one of the short ends starts to lift. Keep pulling it so that it starts to fold in, pressing it along the way and helping to form it into a roll. When the loaf is all rolled, seal up the ends the best you can.

5. Spray crock with nonstick spray, then place the stuffed loaf inside.

6. Cover and cook on Low for 6–7 hours.

7. Let it cool slightly before slicing.

Taco Meatloaf

Tammy Smith, Dorchester, WI

Makes 8 servings

Prep. Time: 20 minutes   ♣   Cooking Time: 4 hours   ♣   Ideal slow-cooker size: oval 5- or 6-qt.

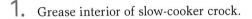

3 eggs, lightly beaten

½ cup crushed tomatoes

¾ cup crushed tortilla chips

I medium onion, finely chopped

2 cloves garlic, minced

3 tsp. taco seasoning

2 tsp. chili powder

I lb. ground beef

I lb. ground pork

½ tsp. salt

¾ tsp. black pepper

1. Grease interior of slow-cooker crock.

2. Make a tinfoil sling for your slow cooker so you can lift the cooked meatloaf out easily. Begin by folding a strip of foil accordion-fashion so that it's about 1½–2 inches wide, and long enough to fit from the top edge of the crock, down inside and up the other side, plus a 2-inch overhang on each side of the cooker. Make a second strip exactly like the first.

3. Place one strip in crock, running from end to end. Place second strip in crock, running from side to side. The strips should form a cross in bottom of the crock.

4. In a large bowl, combine all ingredients well.

5. Shape into a loaf. Place into crock so that the center of loaf sits where the two strips of foil cross.

6. Cover. Cook for 4 hours on Low.

7. Using the foil handles, lift loaf onto platter. Cover to keep warm. Let stand for 10–15 minutes before slicing.

TIP

This is an all-time favorite that I've made for years. Everyone asks for this recipe! My original recipe said to cook 7–8 hours, but 10 hours is even better if you have the time. Warming the hoagie rolls is nice too.

Beef and Pepperoncini Hoagies

Donna Treloar, Muncie, IN

Makes 10 servings (varies with roast size)

Prep. Time: 15 minutes & Cooking Time: 8–10 hours & Ideal slow-cooker size: 5- or 6-qt.

3–5-lb. boneless chuck roast (inexpensive cuts work fine)

16-oz. jar of pepperoncini peppers, mild or medium, depending on your preference

1 clove garlic, minced, or 1 tsp. garlic powder

salt and pepper to taste

hoagie rolls or buns of your choice

20 slices provolone cheese

Variations:

This is excellent as is, but I frequently add chopped onions to Step 7 . . . just because we love onions. You can also add a package of dry Italian dressing mix and a cup or two of beef broth to Steps 7 and 8. Or you can add a package of Lipton Onion Soup mix along with beef and chicken broth. It's hard to hurt this recipe!

Good go-alongs with this recipe:

Sweet potato fries.

1. Grease interior of slow-cooker crock.

2. Trim roast of fat.

3. Salt and pepper to taste, holding over crock.

4. If using garlic powder, sprinkle on all sides of beef over crock. Place beef in crock.

5. If using minced garlic, scatter over beef in crock.

6. If the pepperoncini peppers are whole and have stems, remove peppers from jar and cut up. Reserve liquid.

7. Scatter cut-up peppers over meat.

8. Pour liquid from peppers down alongside of crock interior so you don't wash off the seasonings.

9. Cover. Cook on low 7½–9½ hours, or until beef registers 160°F on an instant-read meat thermometer when stuck in center of roast.

10. Lift roast into a big bowl and shred with two forks.

11. Stir shredded meat back into juices in crock.

12. Cover. Cook another 30 minutes on Low.

13. When ready to serve, use a slotted spoon to drain meat well.

14. Spoon well-drained meat onto a hoagie roll and top each sandwich with 2 slices cheese.

So-Good Sloppy Joes

Judy Diller, Bluffton, OH

Makes 18 servings

Prep. Time: 20 minutes ⚶ *Cooking Time: 4–5 hours* ⚶ *Ideal slow-cooker size: 5- or 6-qt.*

3 lbs. ground beef

1 medium onion, chopped

1 green bell pepper, diced

10¾-oz. can tomato soup

1 cup ketchup (use a lively one if you like some kick)

2 Tbsp. prepared mustard (use a spicy variety if you want some extra zest)

2 Tbsp. apple cider vinegar

1 Tbsp. brown sugar

2 Tbsp. Worcestershire sauce

18 burger rolls

1. Grease interior of slow-cooker crock.

2. If you have time, brown beef in large skillet. Using a slotted spoon, lift beef out of drippings and place in crock. If you don't have time, place beef in crock and use a sturdy spoon to break it up into small clumps.

3. Stir in all remaining ingredients except rolls.

4. Cover. Cook on Low 4–5 hours, or until beef is fully cooked and veggies are as tender as you like them.

5. Serve in rolls. Turn the cooker to Warm and serve the So-Good Sloppy Joes over a several-hour period if you wish.

Stuffed Bell Peppers

Mary Puterbaugh, Elwood, IN

Makes 8 servings

Prep. Time: 20 minutes   ❧   *Cooking Time: 5–11 hours*   ❧   *Ideal slow-cooker size: 6- to 7-qt.*

2 lbs. ground beef, lightly browned

1 large onion, chopped

1 cup cooked rice

2 eggs, beaten

½ cup milk

½ cup ketchup

dash hot pepper sauce

2 tsp. salt

½ tsp. pepper

8 large bell peppers, capped and seeded

1. Combine all ingredients except peppers. Gently pack mixture into peppers. Place in greased slow cooker.

2. Cover. Cook on Low 9–11 hours, or on High 5–6 hours.

Zucchini-Hamburger Bake

Linda Overholt, Abbeville, SC

Makes 6 servings

Prep. Time: 20–30 minutes ⚜ *Cooking Time: 4 hours* ⚜ *Ideal slow-cooker size: 5-qt.*

1 lb. ground beef

1 small onion, chopped

½ tsp. salt

¼ tsp. black pepper

2 cups pizza sauce

4 cups zucchini, peeled or not, and cubed

1½ cups water, *divided*

½ cup instant rice

¾ cup shredded mozzarella cheese

1. Grease interior of slow-cooker crock.

2. If you have time, brown beef and onion together in a skillet. Using a slotted spoon, lift beef and onion out of drippings and place in crock. If you don't have time, place beef in bowl and use a sturdy spoon to break up into small clumps. Mix in onion. Place in crock.

3. Stir in salt and pepper, pizza sauce, zucchini, and ¾ cup water. Mix well.

4. Cover. Cook on Low 3½ hours, or until beef is cooked through and vegetables are as tender as you like them.

5. Stir in rice and remaining water.

6. Cover. Cook on High 20–30 minutes, or until rice is tender.

7. Remove lid. Sprinkle grated cheese over top.

8. Allow to stand until cheese is melted. Then serve.

Vegetarian & Fish Main Dishes

Creamy Mac and Cheese

Renee Hankins, Narvon, PA

Makes 6 servings

Prep. Time: 5 minutes   ❧   Cooking Time: 3–4 hours   ❧   Ideal slow-cooker size: 5-qt.

12 oz. uncooked elbow macaroni

2 cups milk

12-oz. can evaporated milk

1 small onion, chopped

½ tsp. salt

¼ tsp. black pepper

1 cup grated Gouda cheese

1½ cups grated cheddar cheese

1. Grease interior of slow-cooker crock.

2. Mix all ingredients, except Gouda and cheddar cheeses, in crock.

3. Cover. Cook on Low 3–4 hours, or until macaroni are as soft as you like them.

4. Thirty minutes before end of cooking time, stir in cheeses. Cover and continue cooking.

5. If you want a crispy top, or if water has gathered around the edges, uncover during last 30 minutes of cooking time.

"Baked" Macaroni and Cheese

Lorna Rodes, Port Republic, VA

Makes 8 servings

Prep. Time: 30 minutes ⚘ Cooking Time: 3–4 hours ⚘ Ideal slow-cooker size: 4-qt.

8 oz. uncooked elbow macaroni

12-oz. can evaporated milk

½ cup milk

1 tsp. salt

pepper to taste

2 eggs, beaten

3 cups shredded cheese of your choice

4 Tbsp. (½ stick) melted butter

4 slices of your favorite cheese

1. Grease interior of slow-cooker crock.

2. Cook macaroni according to package directions, just until al dente. Drain.

3. Pour barely cooked macaroni into crock. Mix in all remaining ingredients, except slices of cheese.

4. Top with 4 slices of your favorite cheese.

5. Cover. Cook on Low 2–3 hours, just until macaroni are tender but not mushy.

Gluten-Free Vegetarian Lasagna

Hope Comerford, Clinton Township, MI

Makes 6–10 servings

Prep. Time: 20 minutes ⚜ *Cooking Time: 3½–4 hours.* ⚜ *Ideal slow-cooker size: 6- or 7-qt.*

2 24-oz. jars of your favorite pasta sauce, *divided*

10-oz. box of brown rice lasagna noodles

1 cup cottage cheese

1 egg

½ tsp. garlic powder

½ tsp. onion powder

¼ tsp. salt

¼ tsp. oregano

¼ tsp. basil

⅛ tsp. pepper

1 cup chopped zucchini, *divided*

2 cups chopped yellow squash, *divided*

2 cups fresh spinach leaves, *divided*

2–3 cups shredded mozzarella cheese, *divided*

1. Spray crock with nonstick spray.

2. Ladle ½ cup of pasta sauce onto the bottom of the crock and spread around.

3. Lay down 1 layer of lasagna noodles, breaking pieces to fill in smaller spots.

4. Mix the cottage cheese, egg, garlic powder, onion powder, salt, oregano, basil, and pepper.

5. Spread half of the cottage cheese mixture carefully over the layer of noodles in the crock, followed by half of the zucchini, half of the yellow squash, half of the spinach leaves, ⅓ of the remaining pasta sauce, and ⅓ of the mozzarella cheese.

6. Place another layer of lasagna noodles down, then spread the remaining cottage cheese, zucchini, yellow squash, spinach, and ⅓ more of the pasta sauce and mozzarella cheese.

7. Add one last layer of lasagna noodles and spread the remaining pasta sauce and cheese over the top.

8. Cover and cook on Low for 3½–4 hours.

Fresh Veggie Lasagna

Deanne Gingrich, Lancaster, PA

Makes 4–6 servings

Prep. Time: 30 minutes ⚬ *Cooking Time: 4 hours* ⚬ *Ideal slow-cooker size: 4- or 5-qt.*

1½ cups shredded mozzarella cheese

½ cup ricotta cheese

⅓ cup grated Parmesan cheese

1 egg, lightly beaten

1 tsp. dried oregano

¼ tsp. garlic powder

3 cups marinara sauce, *divided*, plus more for serving

1 medium zucchini, diced, *divided*

4 uncooked lasagna noodles

4 cups fresh baby spinach, *divided*

1 cup fresh mushrooms, sliced, *divided*

1. Grease interior of slow-cooker crock.

2. In a bowl, mix together mozzarella, ricotta, and Parmesan cheeses, egg, oregano, and garlic powder. Set aside.

3. Spread ½ cup marinara sauce in crock.

4. Sprinkle with half the zucchini.

5. Spoon ⅓ of cheese mixture over zucchini.

6. Break 2 noodles into large pieces to cover cheese layer.

7. Spread ½ cup marinara over noodles.

8. Top with half the spinach and then half the mushrooms.

9. Repeat layers, ending with cheese mixture, and then sauce. Press layers down firmly.

10. Cover. Cook on Low 4 hours, or until vegetables are as tender as you like them and noodles are fully cooked.

11. Let stand 15 minutes so lasagna can firm up before serving.

Pasta with Tomatoes, Olives, and Two Cheeses

Diane Clement, Rogers, AR

Makes 6–8 servings

Prep. Time: 30 minutes ❧ Cooking Time: 3 hours ❧ Ideal slow-cooker size: 5- or 6-qt.

1½ cups chopped onion

1 tsp. minced garlic

3 28-oz. cans Italian plum tomatoes, drained

2 tsp. dried basil

¼–½ tsp. red pepper flakes, according to the amount of heat you like

2 cups chicken broth

salt and black pepper to taste

1 lb. uncooked penne or rigatoni

3 Tbsp. olive oil

2½ cups Havarti cheese

⅓ cup sliced, pitted, brine-cured olives (such as Kalamata)

⅓ cup grated Parmesan cheese

¼ cup finely chopped fresh basil

1. Grease interior of slow-cooker crock.

2. Place onion, garlic, tomatoes, dried basil, and red pepper flakes in crock. Stir together well, breaking up tomatoes with back of spoon.

3. Stir in chicken broth.

4. Season with salt and pepper.

5. Cover. Cook on High 2 hours.

6. Uncover. Continue cooking on High 1 hour, or until sauce is reduced to the consistency you like.

7. During last 30 minutes of cooking, prepare pasta according to package directions in a large stockpot until al dente.

8. Drain pasta and stir in olive oil. Cover and keep warm.

9. When sauce is done cooking, pour over pasta and toss to blend.

10. Stir in Havarti cheese and allow to melt.

11. Spoon into serving bowl. Top with olives and Parmesan cheese.

12. Sprinkle with fresh basil, then serve immediately.

Double Corn Tortilla Bake

Kathy Keener Shantz, Lancaster, PA

Makes 4 servings

Prep. Time: 15 minutes ❧ *Cooking Time: 2–3 hours* ❧ *Ideal slow-cooker size: 3- or 4-qt.*

8 corn tortillas, *divided*

1½ cups shredded Monterey Jack cheese, *divided*

1 cup corn, fresh, frozen, or canned (drained of water), *divided*

4 green onions, sliced, about ½ cup, *divided*

2 eggs, beaten

1 cup buttermilk

4-oz. can diced green chilies

1. Grease interior of slow-cooker crock.

2. Tear 4 tortillas into bite-sized pieces. Scatter evenly over bottom of crock.

3. Top with half the cheese, half the corn, and half the green onions.

4. Repeat layers.

5. In a mixing bowl, stir together eggs, buttermilk, and chilies. Gently pour over tortilla mixture.

6. Cover. Cook on Low 2–3 hours, or until knife inserted in center comes out clean.

Vegetable Stuffed Peppers

Shirley Hinh, Wayland, IA

Makes 8 servings

Prep. Time: 20 minutes ⚖ Cooking Time: 6–8 hours
Ideal slow-cooker size: 6-qt. (large enough so that all peppers sit on the bottom of the cooker)

4 large green, red, or yellow bell peppers

½ cup quick-cooking rice

¼ cup minced onion

¼ cup sliced black olives

2 tsp. light soy sauce

¼ tsp. black pepper

1 clove garlic, minced

28-oz. can low-sodium whole tomatoes

6-oz. can low-sodium tomato paste

15¼-oz. can corn or kidney beans, drained

1. Cut tops off peppers (reserve) and remove seeds. Stand peppers up in slow cooker.

2. Mix remaining ingredients in a bowl. Stuff peppers. (You'll have leftover filling.)

3. Place pepper tops back on peppers. Pour remaining filling over the stuffed peppers and work down in between the peppers.

4. Cover. Cook on Low 6–8 hours, or until the peppers are done to your liking.

5. If you prefer, you may add ½ cup tomato juice if recipe is too dry.

6. Cut peppers in half and serve.

Salsa Lentils

Karen Stanley, Amherst, VA

Makes 4 servings

Prep. Time: 15 minutes   Cooking Time: 2–4 hours   Ideal slow-cooker size: 4- or 5-qt.

2 cups dry green lentils, picked over for any stones and rinsed

4 cups water

2 cups chopped onions

¼ cup chopped garlic

2 cups salsa, mild, medium, or hot

1–3 jalapeño peppers, seeded and chopped

1¼-oz. pkg. dry taco seasoning

½ tsp. salt

1 cup chopped fresh cilantro

cooked rice or corn chips

chopped lettuce, *optional*

diced fresh tomatoes, *optional*

grated cheese of your choice, *optional*

sour cream, *optional*

1. Grease interior of slow-cooker crock.

2. Place lentils, water, onions, garlic, salsa, jalapeño peppers, taco seasoning, and salt in crock. Stir together until well mixed.

3. Cover. Cook on Low 3–4 hours or on High 2–3 hours, or until lentils are tender.

4. Just before serving, stir in chopped cilantro.

5. Serve over rice or corn chips.

6. Top with remaining ingredients.

Lentil Tacos

Judy Buller, Bluffton, OH

Makes 6 servings

Prep. Time: 20 minutes ♣ Cooking Time: 3–6 hours ♣ Ideal slow-cooker size: 4-qt.

⅛ tsp. garlic powder

¾ cup onions, finely chopped

1 tsp. canola oil

½ lb. dry lentils, picked clean of stones and floaters

1 Tbsp. chili powder

2 tsp. ground cumin

1 tsp. dried oregano

2 cups fat-free, low-sodium chicken broth

1 cup salsa

12 taco shells

shredded lettuce

tomatoes, chopped

shredded, reduced-fat cheddar cheese

fat-free sour cream

taco sauce

1. Sprinkle garlic powder over onions and sauté in oil in skillet until tender. Add lentils and spices. Cook and stir 1 minute.

2. Place lentil mixture and broth in slow cooker.

3. Cover. Cook on Low 3 hours for somewhat-crunchy lentils, or on Low 6 hours for soft lentils.

4. Add salsa.

5. Spoon about ¼ cup into each taco shell. Top with your choice of lettuce, tomatoes, cheese, sour cream, and taco sauce.

TIP

This mixture is also tasty served over rice.

Cherry Tomato Spaghetti Sauce

Beverly Hummel, Fleetwood, PA

Makes 8–10 servings

Prep. Time: 20 minutes ⚜ *Cooking Time: 4–5 hours* ⚜ *Ideal slow-cooker size: 6-qt.*

4 quarts cherry tomatoes

I onion, chopped

2 cloves garlic, minced

3 tsp. sugar

I tsp. dried rosemary

2 tsp. dried thyme

I tsp. dried oregano

I tsp. dried basil

I tsp. salt

½ tsp. coarsely ground black pepper

cooked spaghetti

1. Grease interior of slow-cooker crock.

2. Stem tomatoes and cut them in half. Place in slow cooker.

3. Add chopped onion and garlic to cooker.

4. Stir in sugar, herbs, and seasonings, mixing well.

5. Cover. Cook on Low 4–5 hours, or until the veggies are as tender as you like them.

6. For a thicker sauce, uncover the cooker for the last 30–60 minutes of cooking time.

7. Serve over just-cooked spaghetti.

Slimmed-Down Pasta Sauce

Dolores Kratz, Souderton, PA

Makes 3½ cups sauce, or 4 servings

Prep. Time: 15 minutes ⚬ *Cooking Time: 2–4 hours* ⚬ *Ideal slow-cooker size: 3-qt.*

24-oz. can low-sodium tomato juice
6-oz. can tomato paste
½ cup grated carrots
2 large garlic cloves, mashed
1 tsp. dried oregano leaves, crushed
1 tsp. onion salt
1 medium bay leaf
dash pepper

1. Combine all ingredients in slow cooker.

2. Cover. Cook on low 2–4 hours.

3. Remove bay leaf.

4. Serve over your favorite pasta.

Tex-Mex Luau

Dorothy VanDeest, Memphis, TN

Makes 6 servings

Prep. Time: 20 minutes ⚘ *Cooking Time: 2–3 hours* ⚘ *Ideal slow-cooker size: 3- or 4-qt.*

1½ lbs. frozen firm-textured fish fillets, thawed

2 onions, thinly sliced

2 lemons, *divided*

2 Tbsp. butter, melted

2 tsp. salt

1 bay leaf

4 whole peppercorns

1 cup water

1. Cut fillets into serving portions.

2. Combine onion slices and 1 sliced lemon in butter, along with salt, bay leaf, and peppercorns. Pour into slow cooker.

3. Place fillets on top of onion and lemon slices. Add water.

4. Cover. Cook on High 2–3 hours or until fish is flaky.

5. Before serving, carefully remove fish fillets with slotted spoon. Place on heatproof plate.

6. Sprinkle with juice of half of the second lemon. Garnish with remaining lemon slices.

Herbed Flounder

Dorothy VanDeest, Memphis, TN

Makes 6 servings

Prep. Time: 10 minutes ⚬ *Cooking Time: 2–3 hours* ⚬ *Ideal slow-cooker size: 6-qt.*

2 lbs. flounder fillets (fresh or frozen)

½ tsp. salt

¾ cup chicken broth

2 Tbsp. lemon juice

2 Tbsp. dried chives

2 Tbsp. dried minced onion

½–1 tsp. leaf marjoram

4 Tbsp. fresh parsley, chopped

1. Wipe fish as dry as possible. Cut fish into portions to fit slow cooker.

2. Combine broth and lemon juice. Stir in remaining ingredients.

3. Place a meat rack in the slow cooker. Lay fish on rack. Pour liquid mixture over each portion.

4. Sprinkle with salt.

5. Cover. Cook on High 2–3 hours, or until fish is flaky.

Side Dishes & Vegetables

Barbecued Green Beans

Sharon Timpe, Jackson, WI
Ruth E. Martin, Loysville, PA

Makes 10–12 servings

Prep. Time: 15 minutes ⚬ Cooking Time: 3–4 hours ⚬ Ideal slow-cooker size: 4-qt.

3 14½-oz. cans cut green beans (drain 2 cans completely; reserve liquid from 1 can)

1 small onion, diced

1 cup ketchup

¾ cup brown sugar

4 strips bacon, cooked crisp and crumbled

1. Combine green beans, diced onion, ketchup, and brown sugar in your slow cooker.

2. Add ⅓ cup of reserved bean liquid. Mix gently.

3. Cover and cook on Low 3–4 hours, until beans are tender and heated through. Stir at the end of 2 hours of cooking, if you're home.

4. Pour in a little reserved bean juice if the sauce thickens more than you like.

5. Sprinkle bacon over beans just before serving.

TIP

Use 1½ lbs. fresh green beans instead of canned beans. When using fresh beans, you'll need to increase the cooking time to 5–6 hours on Low depending upon how soft or crunchy you like your beans

Fresh Green Beans

Lizzie Ann Yoder, Hartville, OH

Makes 6–8 servings

Prep. Time: 20 minutes & Cooking Time: 6–24 hours & Ideal slow-cooker size: 4- to 5-qt.

¼ lb. ham, or bacon, pieces

2 lbs. fresh green beans, washed and cut into pieces, or frenched

3–4 cups water

I scant tsp. salt

1. If using bacon, cut it into squares and brown in nonstick skillet. When crispy, drain and set aside.

2. Place all ingredients in slow cooker. Mix together well.

3. Cover and cook on High 6–10 hours, or on Low 10–24 hours, or until beans are done to your liking.

Green Beans with Dill

Rebecca Leichty, Harrisonburg, VA

Makes 8 servings

Prep. Time: 5 minutes ⚓ *Cooking Time: 3–4 hours* ⚓ *Ideal slow-cooker size: 3½- or 4-qt.*

2 qts. fresh cut green beans, or 4 14½-oz. cans cut green beans

2 tsp. beef bouillon granules

½ tsp. dill seed

¼ cup water

1. Spray slow cooker with fat-free cooking spray.

2. Add all ingredients and mix well.

3. Cook on High 3–4 hours, or until beans are done to your liking.

Savory Spinach Salad with Rice

Phyllis Good, Lancaster, PA

Makes 6 servings

Prep. Time: 20 minutes ⚘ *Cooking Time: 2½–3 hours* ⚘ *Chilling Time: 8 hours* ⚘ *Ideal slow-cooker size: 3-qt.*

1 Tbsp. butter

1 Tbsp. sesame oil

1 small onion, chopped

1 cup uncooked long-grain brown rice

2 Tbsp. soy sauce

1½ cups water

1 cup Italian salad dressing

1 tsp. sugar

2 generous cups chopped fresh spinach

2 ribs celery, diced

½ cup spring onions, sliced

3 slices bacon, chopped, fried, and drained

2 hard-boiled eggs, chopped, *optional*

1. Sauté onion in butter and sesame oil over low heat until quite browned, about 15 minutes.

2. Scrape onion and drippings into slow cooker.

3. Add rice, soy sauce, and water. Cover and cook on High for 2½–3 hours, until water is absorbed and rice is still firm.

4. Remove rice mixture to bowl. Stir in Italian dressing and sugar. Refrigerate 8 hours or overnight.

5. Just before serving, stir in spinach, celery, spring onions, bacon, and optional eggs.

Spinach Squares

Phyllis Good, Lancaster, PA

Makes 6 servings

Prep. Time: 15 minutes & Cooking Time: 2½–3 hours & Ideal slow-cooker size: 3- or 4-qt.

3 eggs

1 cup milk

1 cup all-purpose flour

1 tsp. baking powder

½ lb. Monterey Jack cheese, grated

¼ lb. jalapeño Monterey Jack cheese, grated

1½ 10-oz. frozen pkgs. chopped spinach, thawed and squeezed dry, or 1 lb. fresh spinach, chopped

1. Combine eggs, milk, flour, and baking powder in a bowl and stir until a batter forms. Stir in the cheeses and spinach.

2. Spread the mixture into your greased slow cooker.

3. Cook on Low for 2½–3 hours, or until a knife inserted into the center comes out clean.

4. Let it stand for 15 minutes so that the cheeses can firm up before cutting and serving the squares.

Asparagus Bake

Leona M. Slabaugh, Apple Creek, OH

Makes 4–6 servings

Prep. Time: 20 minutes & Cooking Time: 3½–4½ hours & Ideal slow-cooker size: 4-qt.

5 medium potatoes, unpeeled, sliced

1 onion, sliced

salt and pepper

1 cup sliced fresh mushrooms

1 bunch fresh asparagus

3 Tbsp. butter

½–¾ cup grated smoked cheddar cheese

1. In greased slow cooker, layer potatoes and onion. Sprinkle with salt and pepper. Add mushrooms and asparagus. Sprinkle again with salt and pepper.

2. Dot with butter.

3. Cover and cook on Low for 3–4 hours, until potatoes are tender.

4. Uncover and turn to High. Sprinkle with cheese. Cook uncovered an additional 30 minutes as cheese melts and extra moisture evaporates.

Baked Tomatoes

Lizzie Ann Yoder, Hartville, OH

Makes 4 servings

Prep. Time: 10 minutes 🍃 Cooking Time: 45 minutes–1 hour 🍃 Ideal slow-cooker size: 2½- or 3-qt.

2 tomatoes, each cut in half

½ Tbsp. olive oil

½ tsp. parsley, chopped, or ¼ tsp. dry parsley flakes

¼ tsp. dried oregano

¼ tsp. dried basil

1. Place tomato halves in slow cooker sprayed with nonfat cooking spray.

2. Drizzle oil over tomatoes. Sprinkle with remaining ingredients.

3. Cover. Cook on High 45 minutes to 1 hour.

Corn on the Cob

Donna Conto, Saylorsburg, PA

Makes 3–4 servings

Prep. Time: 10 minutes ♣ Cooking Time: 2–3 hours ♣ Ideal slow-cooker size: 5- or 6-qt.

6–8 ears of corn (in husk)
½ cup water

1. Remove silk from corn, as much as possible, but leave husks on.

2. Cut off ends of corn so ears can stand in the cooker.

3. Add water.

4. Cover. Cook on Low 2–3 hours.

Chili Lime Corn on the Cob

Hope Comerford, Clinton Township, MI

Makes 6 servings

Prep. Time: 10 minutes & *Cooking Time: 4 hours* & *Ideal slow-cooker size: 6-qt.*

6 ears of corn, shucked and cleaned

6 Tbsp. butter, room temperature

2 Tbsp. freshly squeezed lime juice

1 tsp. lime zest

2 tsp. chili powder

1 tsp. salt

½ tsp. pepper

1. Tear off six pieces of aluminum foil to fit each ear of corn. Place each ear of corn on a piece of foil.

2. Mix together the butter, lime juice, lime zest, chili powder, salt, and pepper.

3. Divide the butter mixture evenly between the six ears of corn and spread it over the ears of corn. Wrap them tightly with the foil so they don't leak.

4. Place the foil wrapped ears of corn into the crock. Cover and cook on Low for 4 hours.

Spicy Corn Casserole

Beth Nafziger, Lowville, NY

Makes 10 servings

Prep. Time: 20–30 minutes & Cooking Time: 2–3 hours & Ideal slow-cooker size: 4-qt.

¼ stick (2 Tbsp.) butter

1 large onion, chopped

2 medium green bell peppers, chopped

¼ cup flour

2 cups fresh, or frozen, corn

2 cups cooked long-grain brown rice

14½-oz. can low-sodium diced tomatoes with liquid

2 hard-boiled eggs, chopped

2½ cups low-fat shredded sharp cheese

2 Tbsp. Worcestershire sauce

2–3 tsp. hot pepper sauce

½ tsp. salt

½ tsp. pepper

1. In large skillet, melt butter. Sauté onion and peppers until tender.

2. Stir in flour and remove from heat.

3. Place sautéed vegetables in slow cooker. Add all remaining ingredients. Mix together gently.

4. Cover. Cook on Low 2–3 hours.

TIP

If the corn becomes too dry while cooking, add some tomato juice.

Spanish Baked Corn

Phyllis Good, Lancaster, PA

Makes 4–6 servings

Prep. Time: 15–20 minutes & *Cooking Time: 1½–2½ hours* & *Ideal slow-cooker size: 3-qt.*

6 small corn tortillas, *divided*

⅓ cup shredded smoked cheddar or smoked Gouda cheese, *divided*

1 cup shredded Monterey Jack cheese, *divided*

2 cups frozen corn, *divided*

½ cup chopped onion, *divided*

2 eggs, beaten

1¼ cups buttermilk

½ tsp. dry mustard

¼ tsp. dried oregano

4-oz. can diced green chili peppers, *optional*

1. Tear 3 tortillas into bite-sized pieces. Arrange in greased slow cooker.

2. Gently mix the two cheeses in a small bowl.

3. Place half the cheese mixture on top of the torn tortillas.

4. Add half the corn and half the onions. Repeat the layers, starting with the rest of the torn tortillas.

5. In a mixing bowl, stir together eggs, buttermilk, mustard, oregano, and optional chili peppers. Gently pour over tortilla mixture.

6. Cover and cook on High for 1½–2 hours. The middle should be set and the edges browned when the dish is done. If there is too much moisture around the edges, remove the lid and cook an additional 20 minutes on High.

Caponata

Katrine Rose, Woodbridge, VA

Makes 10 servings

Prep. Time: 25–30 minutes ⚘ *Cooking Time: 5–6 hours* ⚘ *Ideal slow-cooker size: 4-qt.*

1 medium-sized eggplant, peeled and
cut into ½-inch cubes

14-oz. can low-sodium diced tomatoes

1 medium-sized onion, chopped

1 red bell pepper, cut into
½-inch pieces

¾ cup low-sodium salsa

¼ cup olive oil

2 Tbsp. capers, drained

3 Tbsp. balsamic vinegar

3 cloves garlic, minced

1¼ tsp. dried oregano

⅓ cup chopped fresh basil

1. Combine all ingredients except basil in slow cooker.

2. Cover. Cook on Low 5–6 hours, or until vegetables are tender.

3. Stir in basil. Serve over slices of toasted French bread.

Mediterranean Eggplant

Willard E. Roth, Elkhart, IN

Makes 8 servings

Prep. Time: 25–30 minutes ⸙ Cooking Time: 5–6 hours ⸙ Ideal slow-cooker size: 5-qt.

1 medium-sized red onion, chopped

2 cloves garlic, crushed

1 cup fresh mushrooms, sliced

2 Tbsp. olive oil

1 eggplant, unpeeled, cubed

2 green bell peppers, coarsely chopped

28-oz. can crushed tomatoes

28-oz. can garbanzos, drained and rinsed

2 Tbsp. fresh rosemary

1 cup fresh parsley, chopped

½ cup Kalamata olives, pitted and sliced

1. Sauté onion, garlic, and mushrooms in olive oil in skillet over medium heat. Transfer to slow cooker coated with nonfat cooking spray.

2. Add eggplant, peppers, tomatoes, garbanzos, rosemary, and parsley to cooker.

3. Cover. Cook on Low 5–6 hours.

4. Stir in olives just before serving.

5. Serve with couscous or polenta.

Eggplant & Zucchini Casserole

Jennifer Dzialowski, Brighton, MI

Makes 6 servings

Prep. Time: 25–30 minutes ☙ *Cooking Time: 5–6 hours* ☙ *Ideal slow-cooker size: 5-qt.*

2 egg whites

1 medium-sized eggplant

1 medium-sized zucchini

1½ cups bread crumbs

1 tsp. garlic powder

1 tsp. low-sodium Italian seasoning

48-oz. jar fat-free, low-sodium spaghetti sauce

8-oz. bag low-fat shredded mozzarella cheese

1. Beat egg whites in small bowl.

2. Slice eggplant and zucchini. Place in separate bowl.

3. Combine in another bowl bread crumbs, garlic powder, and Italian seasoning.

4. Dip sliced veggies in egg white and then in bread crumbs. Layer in slow cooker, pouring sauce and sprinkling cheese over each layer. (Reserve ½ cup cheese). Top with sauce.

5. Cover. Cook on Low 5–6 hours, or until vegetables are tender.

6. Top with remaining cheese during last 15 minutes of cooking.

Variation:

For added flavoring, sprinkle chopped onions and minced garlic over each layer of vegetables.

Zucchini Casserole

Hope Comerford, Clinton Township, MI

Makes 4–6 servings

Prep. Time: 15 minutes   ♣   Cooking Time: 3 hours   ♣   Ideal slow-cooker size: 3-qt.

4 medium zucchini, sliced

1 large yellow onion, sliced in half rings

1 red pepper, sliced

14½-oz. can diced tomatoes

1 tsp. sea salt

1 tsp. Italian seasoning

2 Tbsp. butter

¼ cup shredded Parmesan cheese

1. Spray crock with nonstick spray.

2. In the crock, mix the zucchini, onion, red pepper, diced tomatoes, sea salt, and Italian seasoning.

3. Cut the butter into about 6 pieces and spread them over the top of the contents of the crock.

4. Sprinkle the Parmesan cheese on top.

5. Cover and cook on Low for 3 hours.

Zucchini Special

Louise Stackhouse, Benten, PA

Makes 4 servings

Prep. Time: 20 minutes ⚜ *Cooking Time: 5–6 hours* ⚜ *Ideal slow-cooker size: 3-qt.*

1 medium-to-large zucchini, peeled and sliced

1 medium-sized onion, sliced

1 qt. low-sodium stewed tomatoes with juice, or 2 14½-oz. cans low-sodium stewed tomatoes with juice

¼ tsp. salt

1 tsp. dried basil

8 oz. fat-free mozzarella cheese, shredded

1. Layer zucchini, onion, and tomatoes in slow cooker.

2. Sprinkle with salt and basil.

3. Cover. Cook on Low 5–6 hours.

4. Sprinkle with cheese 15 minutes before end of cooking time.

Zucchini in Sour Cream

Lizzie Ann Yoder, Hartville, OH

Makes 6 servings

Prep. Time: 20 minutes ⚘ *Cooking Time: 1–1½ hours* ⚘ *Ideal slow-cooker size: 3- or 4-qt.*

4 cups unpeeled, sliced zucchini

1 cup fat-free sour cream

¼ cup skim milk

1 cup chopped onions

1 tsp. salt

1 cup grated low-fat sharp cheddar cheese

1. Cook zucchini in microwave on High 2–3 minutes. Turn into slow cooker sprayed with nonfat cooking spray.

2. Combine sour cream, milk, onions, and salt. Pour over zucchini and stir gently.

3. Cover. Cook on Low 1–1½ hours.

4. Sprinkle cheese over vegetables 30 minutes before serving.

Collard Greens with Bacon

Hope Comerford, Clinton Township, MI

Makes 8–10 servings

Prep. Time: 15 minutes ⚬ *Cooking Time: 5–6 hours* ⚬ *Ideal slow-cooker size: 3-qt.*

3 lbs. collard greens, tough stems cut away and washed thoroughly

8 oz. bacon, cooked, chopped

1½ cups chopped onion

4–5 cloves garlic, chopped

1 cup chicken stock

1 cup chopped tomatoes

3 Tbsp. apple cider vinegar

2 tsp. sea salt

¼ tsp. pepper

1 tsp. sugar

1 bay leaf

1. Tear the collard greens into large pieces and place in the crock.

2. Place all of the remaining ingredients in the crock and stir.

3. Cover and cook on Low for 5–6 hours.

Fast and Fabulous Brussels Sprouts

Phyllis Good, Lancaster, PA

Makes 4–6 servings

Prep. Time: 15 minutes ⚹ Cooking Time: 2–5 hours ⚹ Ideal slow-cooker size: 2- or 3-qt.

1 lb. Brussels sprouts, bottoms trimmed off and halved

3 Tbsp. butter, melted

1½ Tbsp. Dijon mustard

¼ tsp. salt

¼ tsp. freshly ground black pepper

¼ cup water

½ tsp. dried tarragon, *optional*

1. Mix all ingredients in slow cooker.

2. Cover and cook on High for 2–2½ hours, or Low for 4–5 hours, until sprouts are just soft. Some of the Brussels sprouts at the sides will get brown and crispy, and this is delicious.

3. Stir well to distribute sauce. Serve hot or warm.

Broccoli and Bell Peppers

Frieda Weisz, Aberdeen, SD

Makes 8 servings

Prep. Time: 20 minutes ⚘ *Cooking Time: 4–5 hours* ⚘ *Ideal slow-cooker size: 3½- or 4-qt.*

2 lbs. fresh broccoli, trimmed and chopped into bite-sized pieces

1 clove garlic, minced

1 green, or red, bell pepper, cut into thin slices

1 onion, cut into slices

4 Tbsp. light soy sauce

½ tsp. salt

dash black pepper

1 Tbsp. sesame seeds, *optional*, as garnish

1. Combine all ingredients except sesame seeds in slow cooker.

2. Cook on Low for 4–5 hours. Top with sesame seeds.

Serving suggestion:

Serve on brown rice.

"Roasted" Summer Veggies

Hope Comerford, Clinton Township, MI

Makes 8 servings

Prep. Time: 25 minutes ❧ *Cooking Time: 4 hours* ❧ *Ideal slow-cooker size: 5- or 6-qt.*

1 large zucchini, sliced into ½-inch chunks

1 large yellow squash, sliced into ½-inch chunks

1 red bell pepper, sliced into strips

1 orange bell pepper, sliced into strips

1 lb. green beans, ends snapped off

1 large red onion, cut into wedges

5 cloves garlic

3 Tbsp. olive oil

2 Tbsp. balsamic vinegar

1 Tbsp. dried basil

1 tsp. sea salt

¼ tsp. pepper

1. Spray crock with nonstick spray.

2. Place all ingredients into crock and stir to combine and coat everything.

3. Cover and cook on Low for 4 hours.

Marinated Summer Vegetables

Hope Comerford, Clinton Township, MI

Makes 8 servings

Prep. Time: 15 minutes ⚜ *Cooking Time: 4 hours* ⚜ *Ideal slow-cooker size: 4-qt.*

1 medium zucchini, sliced into ½-inch chunks

1 medium yellow squash, sliced into ½-inch chunks

1 red bell pepper, sliced into strips

1 orange bell pepper, sliced into strips

1 green bell pepper, sliced into strips

½ cup sliced red onion

16 large fresh button mushrooms

16 cherry tomatoes

¼ cup soy sauce

¼ cup olive oil

¼ cup lemon juice

2 cloves garlic, crushed

1 tsp. salt

⅛ tsp. pepper

1. Place all of the veggies in the crock.

2. In a bowl, mix together the soy sauce, olive oil, lemon juice, garlic, salt, and pepper. Pour this over the veggies.

3. Cover and cook on Low for 4 hours.

Slow Cooker Ratatouille

Nanci Keatley, Salem, OR

Makes 6 servings

Prep. Time: 35–40 minutes ⚹ *Cooking Time: 6–7 hours* ⚹ *Ideal slow-cooker size: 5- or 6-qt.*

I Tbsp. olive oil

I large onion, chopped

6 large cloves garlic, minced

I green bell pepper, cut into strips

I red bell pepper, cut into strips

I medium-sized eggplant, cubed, peeled or not

2 cups mushrooms, thickly sliced

4 tomatoes, cubed

I cup low-sodium tomato puree

¼ cup dry red wine, or wine vinegar

I Tbsp. lemon juice

2 tsp. dried thyme

I tsp. dried oregano

I tsp. ground cumin

½–I tsp. salt

¼–½ tsp. black pepper

4 Tbsp. minced fresh basil

¼ cup fresh parsley, chopped

1. Turn slow cooker on High for 2 minutes.

2. Pour oil into slow cooker and add remaining ingredients, except fresh basil and fresh parsley.

3. Cover. Cook on High 2 hours, then on Low 4–5 hours.

4. Stir in fresh basil. Sprinkle with parsley. Serve.

Vegetable Medley

Deborah Santiago, Lancaster, PA
Judi Manos, West Islip, NY

Makes 8 servings

Prep. Time: 25 minutes ⚬ *Cooking Time: 5–6 hours* ⚬ *Ideal slow-cooker size: 4-qt.*

4 cups peeled and diced potatoes

1½ cups frozen whole-kernel corn

4 medium-sized tomatoes, seeded and diced

1 cup sliced carrots

½ cup chopped onions

¾ tsp. salt

½ tsp. sugar

¾ tsp. dill weed

¼ tsp. black pepper

½ tsp. dried basil

¼ tsp. dried rosemary

1. Combine all ingredients in slow cooker.

2. Cover. Cook on Low 5–6 hours, or until vegetables are tender.

"Stir-Fry" Veggies

Shari and Dale Mast, Harrisonburg, VA

Makes 8 servings

Prep. Time: 30 minutes ⚘ *Cooking Time: 4–10 hours* ⚘ *Ideal slow-cooker size: 6-qt.*

16-oz. bag baby carrots

4 ribs celery, chunked

1 medium-sized onion, diced

14½-oz. can low-sodium Italian-style stewed tomatoes

½ tsp. dried basil

½ tsp. dried oregano

½ tsp. salt

1 large red, or yellow, bell pepper, diced

1 small head cabbage, cut up

1 lb. raw broccoli, cut up

1. Combine carrots, celery, onion, tomatoes, basil, oregano, and salt in slow cooker.

2. Cover. Cook on High 3–4 hours or on Low 6–8 hours, stirring occasionally.

3. Stir in pepper, cabbage, and broccoli.

4. Cook 1 hour more on High, or 2 hours more on Low, stirring occasionally. You may need to add a little water if there is not liquid left on the veggies.

Serving suggestion:

Serve this as a side dish, or as a main dish over hot cooked rice, garnished with Parmesan cheese.

Tofu and Vegetables

Donna Lantgen, Rapid City, SD

Makes 6 servings

Prep. Time: 25–30 minutes   ⚶   *Cooking Time: 6 hours*   ⚶   *Ideal slow-cooker size: 4- or 5-qt.*

16 oz. firm tofu, drained and crumbled

½ cup chopped onion

½ cup chopped celery

2 cups chopped bok choy

2 cups chopped Napa cabbage

½ cup pea pods, cut in half

1. Combine all ingredients in slow cooker.

2. Cook on Low 6 hours.

TIP
I like to serve this with soy sauce on a bed of rice.

Slow-Cooked Baked Beans

Hope Comerford, Clinton Township, MI

Makes 15–20 servings

Soaking time: 12 hours   ❧   Prep. Time: 10 minutes
Cooking Time: 12 or more hours   ❧   Ideal slow-cooker size: 6-qt.

2 lbs. navy beans

12 oz. salt pork, chopped into small strips, *divided*

1 large onion, chopped, *divided*

¾ cup dark brown sugar

1 cup ketchup

3 Tbsp. mustard

7 cups water

TIP

If you can't find salt pork, use thick cut bacon instead.

1. Sort the beans to make sure there are no rocks or bad beans.

2. Soak the beans in water for 12 or more hours, with enough water to cover them plus four inches.

3. Spray crock with nonstick spray.

4. Place half of the salt pork at the bottom, then half the beans, then half the onion.

5. In a bowl, mix together the brown sugar, ketchup, and mustard. Pour half of this over the contents of the crock.

6. Place the rest of the salt pork into the crock, then the remaining beans, onions, and sauce.

7. Pour in the 7 cups of water.

8. Cover and cook on Low for 12 or more hours. You will know these are done when your mixture has turned nice and brown and has thickened.

Barbecued Baked Beans

Mary Ann Bowman, East Earl, PA

Makes 8–10 servings

Prep. Time: 10 minutes ♣ *Cooking Time: 3–4 hours* ♣ *Ideal slow-cooker size: 4-qt.*

2 16-oz. cans baked beans,
your choice of variety

2 15-oz. cans kidney or pinto beans,
or one of each, drained

½ cup brown sugar

1 cup ketchup

1 onion, chopped

1. Combine all ingredients in slow cooker. Mix well.

2. Cover and cook on Low 3–4 hours, or until heated through.

Best Baked Beans

Nadine Martinitz, Salina, KS

Makes 8–10 servings

Prep. Time: 15 minutes ⚶ *Cooking Time: 2–6 hours* ⚶ *Ideal slow-cooker size: 6-qt.*

8 strips bacon, diced
1 small onion, chopped
5 15-oz. cans pork and beans
2 Tbsp. Worcestershire sauce
⅓ cup brown sugar
½ cup molasses
½ cup ketchup
dash ground cloves

1. Sauté bacon in skillet until crisp. Remove bacon but retain drippings in skillet.

2. Brown chopped onion in drippings until translucent.

3. Combine all ingredients in slow cooker. Stir well.

4. Cover. Cook on Low 5–6 hours, or on High 2–3 hours.

American Beans

Jane Geigley, Lancaster, PA

Makes 4–6 servings

Prep. Time: 30 minutes & *Cooking Time: 2 hours* & *Ideal slow-cooker size: 3-qt.*

1 lb. ground beef, browned
16-oz. can pork and beans
16-oz. can kidney beans
1 qt. tomato juice
1 pt. corn
½ cup brown sugar
2 Tbsp. mustard
chili powder to taste
1 tsp. salt
1 tsp. pepper

1. Pour each ingredient into slow cooker.

2. Stir and cook on High for 2 hours.

Serving suggestion:

Serve over baked potatoes or cornbread.

Ranch Beans

Jo Zimmerman, Lebanon, PA

Makes 8–10 servings

Prep. Time: 10 minutes ⚶ Cooking Time: 3–4 hours ⚶ Ideal slow-cooker size: 3-qt.

16-oz. can kidney beans, rinsed and drained

16-oz. can pork and beans

15-oz. can lima beans, rinsed and drained

14-oz. can cut green beans, drained

12-oz. bottle chili sauce

⅔ cup brown sugar, packed

1 small onion, chopped

1. Combine all ingredients in slow cooker. Mix.
2. Cover and cook on High 3–4 hours.

Slow-Simmered Kidney Beans

Frances Kruba, Baltimore, MD

Makes 16 servings

Prep. Time: 20 minutes ⚙ *Cooking Time: 6–8 hours* ⚙ *Ideal slow-cooker size: 5-qt.*

6 bacon strips, diced

½ lb. smoked sausage, chopped

3 16-oz. cans kidney beans, rinsed and drained

28-oz. can diced tomatoes, drained

2 medium red bell peppers, chopped

1 large onion, chopped

1 cup ketchup

½ cup brown sugar, packed

¼ cup honey

¼ cup molasses

1 Tbsp. Worcestershire sauce

1 tsp. salt

¼ tsp. ground pepper

1 tsp. dry mustard

2 medium unpeeled red apples, cored and cut into ½-inch pieces

1. Fry bacon in skillet. Transfer bacon and drippings to slow cooker.

2. Add rest of ingredients to cooker except apples.

3. Cover and cook on Low for 4–6 hours.

4. Stir in apples. Cover and cook on Low 2 more hours.

Twice-Baked Potatoes

Hope Comerford, Clinton Township, MI

Makes 4 servings

Prep. Time: 15 minutes & Cooking Time: 8 hours 35 minutes & Ideal slow-cooker size: 6-qt.

4 medium-large russet potatoes, washed well and dried

olive oil

sea salt

¼ cup milk

¼ cup plain nonfat Greek yogurt

1 cup shredded cheddar cheese

1½ tsp. salt

¼ tsp. pepper

3 Tbsp. chopped chives or green onions

4 bacon slices, cooked and crumbled

1. Pierce each potato with a fork or knife all over.

2. Rub each potato with olive oil and coat with sea salt, then place them in the crock.

3. Cover and cook on Low for 8 hours or until the potatoes are very tender when poked with a fork.

4. Remove the potatoes and let them cool for 3–5 minutes.

5. Cut each potato in half, then scoop out most of the potato, leaving about ⅛-inch of potato in the skin.

6. Mix the scooped-out potato with the milk, yogurt, shredded cheddar cheese, salt, and pepper. Mash it up very well.

7. Spoon the potato mixture in the potato shells then place them back into the crock.

8. Cover and cook on High for 35 minutes.

9. Remove the potatoes from the crock and top them with the chives and bacon before serving.

Dilly Mashed Potatoes with Spinach

Phyllis Good, Lancaster, PA

Makes 6–8 servings

Prep. Time: 25 minutes ⚶ *Cooking Time: 4–6 hours and then 3–4 hours* ⚶ *Ideal slow-cooker size: 5-qt.*

6 medium-sized potatoes

I cup water

I cup sour cream, or Greek yogurt, at room temperature

5 Tbsp. butter, at room temperature

4 oz. cream cheese, at room temperature

1¼ tsp. dill weed

1½ tsp. salt

⅛ tsp. pepper

2 spring onions, chopped

10-oz. box frozen chopped spinach, thawed and squeezed dry

1. Peel some or all of the potatoes. Cube. Place in slow cooker with water.

2. Cover and cook on Low for 4–6 hours, until potatoes are tender. Drain.

3. Place potatoes in mixing bowl. Add sour cream or yogurt, butter, cream cheese, dill, salt, and pepper.

4. Whip well with electric mixer.

5. Fold in spring onions and spinach.

6. Place mixture in lightly greased slow cooker, smoothing top.

7. Cook on Low for 3–4 hours.

German Potato Salad

Hope Comerford, Clinton Township, MI

Makes 6 servings

Prep. Time: 20 minutes & Cooking Time: 3 hours & Ideal slow-cooker size: 4-qt.

1 ½ lbs. red potatoes, coarsely chopped

1 medium onion, chopped

2 slices cooked bacon, chopped

1 cup chopped celery

¼ cup apple cider vinegar

2 Tbsp. whole grain mustard

1 Tbsp. olive oil

½ tsp. sea salt

¼ tsp. pepper

1 Tbsp. cornstarch

1. Place potatoes, onion, bacon, and celery in crock.

2. In a small bowl, combine the apple cider vinegar, mustard, olive oil, salt, pepper and cornstarch. Pour this over the contents of the crock and stir.

3. Cover and cook on Low for 8 hours.

Garlicky Potatoes

Donna Lantgen, Rapid City, SD

Makes 6 servings

Prep. Time: 15–20 minutes ⚘ *Cooking Time: 5–6 hours* ⚘ *Ideal slow-cooker size: 3½-qt.*

6 potatoes, peeled and cubed

6 cloves garlic, minced

¼ cup dried minced onion, or one medium onion, chopped

2 Tbsp. olive oil

1. Combine all ingredients in slow cooker.

2. Cook on Low 5–6 hours, or until potatoes are soft but not turning brown.

Lemon Red Potatoes

Joyce Shackelford, Green Bay, WI

Makes 6 servings

Prep. Time: 15–20 minutes ♣ Cooking Time: 2½–3 hours ♣ Ideal slow-cooker size: 4-qt.

1½ lbs. medium-sized red potatoes
¼ cup water
2 Tbsp. butter, melted
1 Tbsp. lemon juice
3 Tbsp. snipped fresh chives
chopped fresh parsley
1 tsp. salt
½ tsp. black pepper

1. Cut a strip of peel from around the middle of each potato. Place potatoes and water in slow cooker.

2. Cover. Cook on High 2½–3 hours.

3. Drain.

4. Combine butter, lemon juice, chives, and parsley. Pour over potatoes. Toss to coat.

5. Season with salt and pepper.

Baked Potatoes

Mary Jane Musser, Manheim, PA

Makes 6 servings

Prep. Time: 5–10 minutes ⚜ *Cooking Time: 3–8 hours* ⚜ *Ideal slow-cooker size: 4- or 5-qt.*

6 medium-sized baking potatoes
nonfat cooking spray

1. Prick potatoes with fork.

2. Coat each potato with cooking spray. Place potatoes in slow cooker.

3. Cover. Cook on Low 6–8 hours or on High 3–4 hours, or until potatoes jag tender and are not browned.

Desserts & Breads

Gluten-Free Four Berry Cobbler

Hope Comerford, Clinton Township, MI

Makes 6 servings

Prep. Time: 10 minutes & Cooking Time: 4–5 hours & Ideal slow-cooker size: 3-qt.

½ cup sliced strawberries

½ cup blueberries

½ cup blackberries

½ cup raspberries

1 cup gluten-free Bisquick

½ cup turbinado sugar

1 cup milk

½ cup coconut oil, melted

1. Spray crock with nonstick spray.

2. Place berries in the crock.

3. In a bowl, mix together the Bisquick, turbinado sugar, and milk. Pour this over the top of the berries.

4. Pour the melted coconut oil over the top of the Bisquick mixture.

5. Cover and cook on Low for 4–5 hours.

Serving suggestion:

Serve over vanilla ice cream.

Black and Blue Cobbler

Renee Shirk, Mount Joy, PA

Makes 6 servings

Prep. Time: 20 minutes & Cooking Time: 2–2½ hours & Ideal slow-cooker size: 5-qt.

1 cup flour
1 ½ cups sugar, *divided*
1 tsp. baking powder
¼ tsp. salt
¼ tsp. ground cinnamon
¼ tsp. ground nutmeg
2 eggs, beaten
2 Tbsp. milk
2 Tbsp. vegetable oil
2 cups fresh, or frozen, blueberries
2 cups fresh, or frozen, blackberries
¾ cup water
1 tsp. grated orange peel

1. Combine flour, ¾ cup sugar, baking powder, salt, cinnamon, and nutmeg.

2. Combine eggs, milk, and oil. Stir into dry ingredients until moistened.

3. Spread the batter evenly over bottom of greased slow cooker.

4. In saucepan, combine berries, water, orange peel, and remaining ¾ cup sugar. Bring to boil. Remove from heat and pour over batter. Cover.

5. Cook on High 2–2½ hours, or until toothpick inserted into batter comes out clean. Turn off cooker.

6. Uncover and let stand 30 minutes before serving.

Serving suggestion:

Spoon from cooker and serve with whipped topping or ice cream if desired.

Blueberry Bliss Dump Cake

Hope Comerford, Clinton Township, MI

Makes 8 servings

Prep. Time: 10 minutes ⚗ *Cooking Time: 5–6 hours* ⚗ *Ideal slow-cooker size: 3-qt*

2 cups blueberries

2 Tbsp. orange zest

1 Tbsp. fresh orange juice

½ cup turbinado sugar

¼ cup cornstarch

15-oz. box gluten-free yellow cake mix

¼ cup softened coconut oil

4 Tbsp. (½ stick) butter, cut into slices

1. Spray crock with nonstick spray or line with parchment paper.

2. Dump blueberries, orange zest, orange juice, turbinado sugar, and cornstarch into crock and mix.

3. Pour yellow cake over the top of the contents of the crock.

4. Place the coconut oil and slices of butter all over the top of the cake mix.

5. Cover and secure paper towel under the lid to absorb the moisture. Cook on Low for 5–6 hours.

Cherry Berry Cobbler

Hope Comerford, Clinton Township, MI

Makes 6–8 servings

Prep. Time: 15–20 minutes ❧ *Cooking Time: 1½–3 hours* ❧ *Ideal slow-cooker size: 3- to 5-qt.*

8 Tbsp. (1 stick) butter, melted

1 cup flour

1 cup milk

1 cup turbinado sugar

2 tsp. baking powder

¼ tsp. salt

1 cup blackberries

1 cup blueberries

1 cup cherries, pitted

1. Spray crock with nonstick spray.

2. In a bowl, mix together the butter, flour, milk, turbinado sugar, baking powder, and salt. Pour batter into crock.

3. Arrange the fruit on top of batter.

4. Cover and cook on High 1½–3 hours. It's finished when the middle is set and juice is bubbling at the edges.

Sour Cherry Cobbler

Margaret W. High, Lancaster, PA

Makes 6–8 servings

Prep. Time: 20 minutes ❧ Cooking Time: 2 hours ❧ Ideal slow-cooker size: 6-qt.

½ cup whole wheat flour

¾ cup all-purpose flour, *divided*

l Tbsp. sugar, plus ⅔ cup sugar, *divided*

l tsp. baking powder

¼ tsp. salt

¼ tsp. ground cinnamon

¼ tsp. almond extract

l egg

¼ cup milk

2 Tbsp. melted butter

4 cups pitted sour cherries, thawed and drained if frozen

TIP

Cobblers are wonderful served warm with vanilla ice cream, whipped cream, or custard sauce.

1. In mixing bowl, combine whole wheat flour and ½ cup all-purpose flour. Mix in 1 Tbsp. sugar, baking powder, salt, and cinnamon.

2. Separately, combine almond extract, egg, milk, and butter. Stir into dry ingredients just until moistened.

3. Spread batter in bottom of greased slow cooker.

4. Separately, mix remaining ¼ cup flour with ⅔ cup sugar. Add cherries. Sprinkle cherry mixture evenly over batter in slow cooker.

5. Cover and cook on High 2 hours or until lightly browned at edges and juice is bubbling from cherries.

Variations:

Use blueberries instead of sour cherries. Reduce sugar to ½ cup and use vanilla extract instead of almond.

Strawberries and Cream Dump Cake

Hope Comerford, Clinton Township, MI

Makes 8 servings

Prep. Time: 10 minutes ⚇ *Cooking Time: 5–6 hours* ⚇ *Ideal slow-cooker size: 5-qt.*

4 cups strawberries, quartered

1 cup gluten-free flour blend

1 cup turbinado sugar, *divided*

8 oz. cream cheese, softened

15-oz. box gluten-free yellow cake mix

¼ cup softened coconut oil

4 Tbsp. (½ stick) butter, sliced

1. Spray crock with nonstick spray or line with parchment paper.

2. Dump the strawberries, flour, and ½ cup of the turbinado sugar in the crock and stir.

3. Mix together the cream cheese and remaining ½ cup turbinado sugar and spoon it over the top of the strawberries.

4. Sprinkle the cake mix over the contents of the crock.

5. Spoon the coconut oil over the top of the cake mix and place the pieces of butter all around as well.

6. Cover the crock with a paper towel under the lid to absorb moisture. Cook on Low for 5–6 hours.

Country Apples

Betty K. Drescher, Quakertown, PA

Makes 8 servings

Prep. Time: 25 minutes ☙ *Cooking Time: 4–6 hours* ☙ *Ideal slow-cooker size: 2½-qt.*

4–5 cups apples, peeled and sliced

2 Tbsp. flour

¼ cup white sugar

⅓ cup raisins

¼ tsp. ground cinnamon

⅔ cup dry oatmeal, rolled or quick

I cup water

2 Tbsp. butter, melted

⅓ cup brown sugar

1. Coat apples in flour and white sugar. Stir in raisins, cinnamon, and oatmeal.

2. Pour water into slow cooker. Add apple mix.

3. Pour melted butter over apples. Sprinkle with brown sugar.

4. Cover. Cook on Low 4–6 hours.

Serving suggestion:

Serve over vanilla ice cream as a dessert, over oatmeal for breakfast, or use as a filling for crepes.

Apple Crisp

Mary Jane Musser, Manheim, PA

Makes 6 servings

Prep. Time: 15–20 minutes ❧ *Cooking Time: 2–4 hours* ❧ *Ideal slow-cooker size: 3-qt.*

6 cups peeled, cored, and sliced cooking apples

½ cup dry quick oatmeal

½ cup brown sugar

½ cup flour

1 Tbsp. butter, softened

½ tsp. ground cinnamon

1. Place apples in slow cooker sprayed with nonfat cooking spray.

2. Combine remaining ingredients in mixing bowl until crumbly.

3. Sprinkle mixture over apples.

4. Cover. Cook on Low 4 hours or on High 2 hours.

Peach Cobbler

Phyllis Good, Lancaster, PA

Makes 8 servings

Prep. Time: 20 minutes ❧ Cooking Time: 3–4 hours ❧ Ideal slow-cooker size: 5-qt.

3–4 cups sliced peaches
⅓ cup sugar
¼ cup brown sugar
dash nutmeg
dash cinnamon
8 Tbsp. (1 stick) butter
½ cup sugar
¾ cup flour
2 tsp. baking powder
¾ cup milk

1. Grease interior of slow-cooker crock.

2. Mix together in a good-sized bowl the peaches, ⅓ cup sugar, brown sugar, nutmeg, and cinnamon. Set aside to macerate.

3. Melt butter, or place in slow-cooker crock turned on High and let it melt there.

4. Meanwhile, stir together remaining ingredients in a bowl—½ cup sugar, flour, baking powder, and milk—until smooth.

5. When butter is melted, make sure it covers the bottom of the crock. Spoon batter evenly over butter in crock, but don't stir.

6. Spoon sugared peaches over batter.

7. Cover. Bake on High 3–4 hours, or until firm in middle and bubbly around the edges.

8. Uncover carefully so condensation from inside of lid doesn't drip on the cobbler. Remove crock from cooker.

Serving suggestion:
Serve warm with milk or ice cream.

Just Peachy

Betty B. Dennison, Grove City, PA

Makes 4–6 servings

Prep. Time: 2–3 minutes   ⚮   *Cooking Time: 4–5 hours*   ⚮   *Ideal slow-cooker size: 3-qt.*

4 cups sliced peaches, fresh or canned (if using canned peaches, reserve the juice)

⅔ cup rolled dry oats

⅓ cup all-purpose baking mix

½ cup sugar

½ cup brown sugar

½ tsp. cinnamon, *optional*

½ cup water, or reserved peach juice

1. Spray inside of slow cooker with nonstick cooking spray.

2. Place peaches in slow cooker.

3. In a bowl, mix together all dry ingredients. When blended, stir in water or juice until well mixed.

4. Spoon batter into cooker and stir into peaches, just until blended.

5. Cover and cook on Low 4–5 hours.

6. Serve warm with vanilla ice cream or frozen yogurt.

Quick Yummy Peaches

Willard E. Roth, Elkhart, IN

Makes 6 servings

Prep. Time: 10 minutes ❧ *Cooking Time: 5 hours* ❧ *Ideal slow-cooker size: 3½-qt.*

⅓ cup buttermilk baking mix

⅔ cup dry quick oats

½ cup brown sugar

1 tsp. cinnamon

4 cups sliced peaches (canned or fresh)

½ cup peach juice, or water

1. Mix baking mix, oats, brown sugar, and cinnamon together in greased slow cooker.

2. Stir in peaches and peach juice.

3. Cook on Low for at least 5 hours. (If you like a drier cobbler, remove lid for last 15–30 minutes of cooking.)

Serving suggestion:

Serve with frozen yogurt or ice cream.

Peaches and Pudding Crisp

Phyllis Good, Lancaster, PA

Makes 8 servings

Prep. Time: 20 minutes   ❧   Cooking Time: 3–4 hours   ❧   Ideal slow-cooker size: 5-qt.

5–6 cups peaches, fresh or canned

½ cup peach juice or syrup

2 small pkgs. instant vanilla pudding, *divided*

½ cup brown sugar

Topping:

1 cup flour

1½ cups dry oatmeal, quick or rolled

½ cup brown sugar

8 Tbsp. (1 stick) butter, melted

¾ tsp. salt

2 tsp. cinnamon

reserved dry instant vanilla pudding

1. Grease interior of slow-cooker crock.

2. Combine peaches, their syrup or juice, 2 Tbsp. dry pudding mix, and brown sugar in good-sized mixing bowl. Set aside remaining dry pudding mix.

3. Place in slow-cooker crock.

4. Combine all topping ingredients until well blended and crumbly. Sprinkle over peach mixture.

5. Cover. Bake on High 2½–3½ hours, or until firm in middle and bubbly around the edges.

6. Remove lid carefully, tilting it quickly away from yourself so that water from the inside of the lid doesn't drip on the crisp.

7. Continue baking 30 more minutes so crisp dries out on top.

8. Remove crock from cooker and place on baking rack to cool. Serve when warm or at room temperature.

TIP

I like the crisp to be crunchy, and it won't get brown on top in a slow cooker. So I like to run the finished dish under the broiler for just a minute or two till it's properly brown and crunchy. That, against the soft peaches— yum!

Pineapple Upside-Down Cake

Vera M. Kuhns, Harrisonburg, VA

Makes 10 servings

Prep. Time: 20 minutes ⚬ *Cooking Time: 4–5 hours* ⚬ *Ideal slow-cooker size: 4-qt.*

8 Tbsp. (1 stick) butter, or margarine, melted

1 cup brown sugar

1 medium-sized can pineapple slices, drained, reserving juice

6–8 maraschino cherries

1 box dry yellow cake mix

1. Combine butter and brown sugar. Spread over bottom of well-greased cooker.

2. Add pineapple slices and place cherries in the center of each one.

3. Prepare cake batter according to package directions, using pineapple juice for part of liquid. Spoon cake batter into cooker over top of fruit.

4. Cover cooker with 2 tea towels and then with its own lid. Cook on High 1 hour, and then on Low 3–4 hours.

Upside-Down Chocolate Pudding Cake

Sarah Herr, Goshen, IN

Makes 8 servings

Prep. Time: 15 minutes 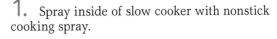 *Cooking Time: 2–3 hours* ❧ *Ideal slow-cooker size: 3½-qt.*

1 cup dry all-purpose baking mix

1 cup sugar, *divided*

3 Tbsp. unsweetened cocoa powder, plus ⅓ cup, *divided*

½ cup milk

1 tsp. vanilla extract

1⅔ cups hot water

1. Spray inside of slow cooker with nonstick cooking spray.

2. In a bowl, mix together baking mix, ½ cup sugar, 3 Tbsp. cocoa powder, milk, and vanilla. Spoon batter evenly into slow cooker.

3. In a clean bowl, mix remaining ½ cup sugar, ⅓ cup cocoa powder, and hot water together. Pour over batter in slow cooker. Do not stir.

4. Cover and cook on High 2–3 hours, or until toothpick inserted in center of cakey part comes out clean.

TIP

The batter will rise to the top and turn into cake. Underneath will be a rich chocolate pudding.

Chocolate Mud Cake

Marci Baum, Annville, PA

Makes 8 servings

Prep. Time: 20 minutes ⚬ Cooking Time: 1–2 hours
Cooling Time: 25 minutes ⚬ Ideal slow-cooker size: 4-qt.

I cup flour

2 tsp. baking powder

2 Tbsp. butter

2 oz. semisweet chocolate, or ⅓ cup chocolate chips

I cup sugar, *divided*

3 Tbsp. plus ⅓ cup Dutch-processed cocoa

I Tbsp. vanilla extract

¼ tsp. salt

⅓ cup skim milk

I egg yolk

⅓ cup brown sugar

I ½ cups hot water

1. Coat inside of slow cooker with nonfat cooking spray.

2. In mixing bowl, whisk together flour and baking powder. Set aside.

3. In large microwave-safe mixing bowl, melt butter and chocolate in microwave. Mix well.

4. Whisk in ⅔ cup sugar, 3 Tbsp. cocoa, vanilla, salt, milk, and egg yolk.

5. Add flour mixture. Stir until thoroughly mixed.

6. Pour batter into slow cooker. Spread evenly.

7. Whisk together remaining sugar, brown sugar, cocoa, and hot water until sugar is dissolved. Pour over batter in slow cooker. Do not stir.

8. Cover. Cook on High 1–2 hours. The cake will be very moist and floating on a layer of molten chocolate when it's done. You'll know it is done cooking when nearly all the cake is set and its edges begin to pull away from the sides of the pot.

9. Turn off slow cooker and remove lid. Try not to let condensed steam from the lid drip onto the cake.

10. Let cool for 25 minutes before cutting and spooning onto individual plates.

Peanut Butter and Hot Fudge Cake

Sara Wilson, Blairstown, MO

Makes 6 servings

Prep. Time: 10 minutes ☙ *Cooking Time: 2–3 hours* ☙ *Ideal slow-cooker size: 4-qt.*

½ cup flour

¾ cup sugar, *divided*

¾ tsp. baking powder

⅓ cup milk

1 Tbsp. oil

½ tsp. vanilla extract

¼ cup peanut butter

3 Tbsp. unsweetened cocoa powder

1 cup boiling water

1. Combine flour, ¼ cup sugar, and baking powder. Add milk, oil, and vanilla. Mix until smooth. Stir in peanut butter. Pour into slow cooker.

2. Mix together ½ cup sugar and cocoa powder. Gradually stir in boiling water. Pour mixture over batter in slow cooker. Do not stir.

3. Cover and cook on High 2–3 hours, or until toothpick inserted comes out clean.

Serving suggestion:

Serve warm and with vanilla ice cream.

Banana Chocolate Chip Bars

Carol Huber, Austin, TX

Makes 12–15 servings

Prep. Time: 20 minutes ♣ Cooking Time: 2–3 hours ♣ Ideal slow-cooker size: 6- or 7-qt. oval

12 Tbsp. (1½ sticks) butter, softened

⅔ cup granulated sugar

⅔ cup brown sugar

2 eggs

1 tsp. vanilla extract

3 ripe bananas, mashed

2 cups flour

2 tsp. baking powder

½ tsp. salt

12-oz. pkg. semisweet chocolate chips

1. Grease a 9x5-inch or 8x4-inch loaf pan that will either hang on the edges of your oval slow-cooker crock, or will sit down in the slow-cooker crock on metal jar rings or a small trivet.

2. In a good-sized mixing bowl, cream together butter and sugars.

3. Add eggs and vanilla. Mix well.

4. Stir in mashed bananas and stir well.

5. In a medium bowl, sift together flour, baking powder, and salt.

6. Stir dry ingredients into creamed mixture.

7. Stir in chocolate chips.

8. Pour into greased loaf pan.

9. Suspend pan on edges of slow-cooker crock, or place on trivet or jar rings on bottom of crock.

10. Vent slow-cooker lid at one end by propping it open with a wooden spoon handle or chopstick.

11. Cook on High 2–3 hours, or until toothpick inserted in center comes out clean.

12. Uncover pan and remove from cooker. Let cool before slicing into bars.

Mama's Rice Pudding

Donna Barnitz, Jenks, OK
Shari Jensen, Fountain, CO

Makes 4–6 servings

Prep. Time: 5 minutes ❧ *Cooking Time: 6–7 hours* ❧ *Ideal slow-cooker size: 4-qt.*

½ cup white rice, uncooked
½ cup sugar
1 tsp. vanilla extract
1 tsp. lemon extract
1 cup plus 2 Tbsp. milk
1 tsp. butter
2 eggs, beaten
1 tsp. cinnamon
½ cup raisins
1 cup whipping cream whipped
nutmeg

1. Combine all ingredients except whipped cream and nutmeg in slow cooker. Stir well.

2. Cover pot. Cook on Low 6–7 hours, until rice is tender and milk absorbed. Be sure to stir once every 2 hours during cooking.

3. Pour into bowl. Cover with plastic wrap and chill.

4. Before serving, fold in whipped cream and sprinkle with nutmeg.

Just Rice Pudding

Audrey L. Kneer, Williamsfield, IL

Makes 10 servings

Prep. Time: 10–15 minutes ❧ *Cooking Time: 2½ hours* ❧ *Ideal slow-cooker size: 5-qt.*

I cup long-grain white rice, uncooked

I cup sugar

9 cups skim milk, *divided*

¾ cup fat-free, cholesterol-free egg product

2 tsp. vanilla extract

¼ tsp. salt

¼ tsp. ground nutmeg, or cinnamon

1. Combine rice, sugar, and 8 cups skim milk in slow cooker.

2. Cover. Cook on High 2 hours, or just until rice is tender.

3. Beat together egg substitute, 1 cup skim milk, vanilla, and salt. Add to slow cooker. Stir.

4. Cover. Cook on High 25–30 minutes.

5. Sprinkle with nutmeg or cinnamon and serve warm.

Tapioca

Ruth Ann Hoover, New Holland, PA
Sharon Anders, Alburtis, PA
Pat Unternahrer, Wayland, IA

Makes 10–12 servings

Prep. Time: 5–10 minutes ☙ *Cooking Time: 3 hours and 20 minutes*
Chilling Time: 4–5 hours ☙ *Ideal slow-cooker size: 3-qt.*

2 qts. whole milk

1¼ cups sugar

1 cup dry small pearl tapioca

4 eggs

1 tsp. vanilla extract

whipped topping, *optional*

1. Combine milk and sugar in slow cooker, stirring until sugar is dissolved as well as possible. Stir in tapioca.

2. Cover and cook on High 3 hours.

3. In a small mixing bowl, beat eggs slightly. Beat in vanilla and about 1 cup hot milk from slow cooker. When well mixed, stir into slow cooker.

4. Cover and cook on High 20 more minutes.

5. Chill. Serve with whipped topping if you wish.

Variations:

1. For a less stiff pudding, use only 3 eggs and/ or only ¾ cup small pearl tapioca.
—Susan Kasting, Jenks, OK and Karen Stoltzfus, Alto, MI

2. For an airier pudding, beat chilled pudding with a rotary beater until fluffy. Fold in an 8-oz. container of whipped topping.

—Evelyn Page, Lance Creek, WY

3. Top chilled pudding with a crushed or broken chocolate candy bar. Or serve the tapioca warm without any topping.

—Karen Stoltzfus, Alto, MI

4. Top chilled pudding with cut-up fruit or berries of your choice (peaches, strawberries, or blueberries are especially good).

—Virginia Eberly, Loysville, PA

Tapioca Salad

Karen Ashworth, Duenweg, MO

Makes 10–12 servings

Prep. Time: 10 minutes & Cooking Time: 3 hours & Ideal slow-cooker size: 4½-qt.

10 Tbsp. large pearl tapioca
½ cup sugar or to taste
dash salt
4 cups water
1 cup grapes, cut in half
1 cup crushed pineapple
1 cup whipped cream

1. Mix together tapioca, sugar, salt, and water in slow cooker.

2. Cook on High 3 hours, or until tapioca pearls are almost translucent.

3. Cool thoroughly in refrigerator.

4. Stir in remaining ingredients.

Serving suggestion:
   Serve cold.

Variation:
   Add 1 small can mandarin oranges, drained, when adding rest of fruit.

Pineapple Sauce

Elizabeth L. Richards, Rapid City, SD

Makes 8 servings

Prep. Time: 10 minutes   Cooking Time: 2 hours   Ideal slow-cooker size: 3-qt.

4 cups apple juice

15-oz. can light crushed pineapples, undrained

1½ cups golden raisins

½ tsp. ground cinnamon

½ tsp. ground allspice

½ cup sugar

¼ cup cornstarch

1. Combine all ingredients in slow cooker. Mix well.

2. Cover. Cook on High 2 hours.

Serving suggestion:

Serve as a topping for dessert, as topping for baked ham, or as a side dish during holidays.

Rhubarb Sauce

Esther Porter, Minneapolis, MN

Makes 4–6 servings

Prep. Time: 10 minutes ⚜ *Cooking Time: 4–5 hours* ⚜ *Ideal slow-cooker size: 1½-qt.*

1 ½ lbs. rhubarb
⅛ tsp. salt
½ cup water
½–⅔ cup sugar

1. Cut rhubarb into ½-inch slices.

2. Combine all ingredients in slow cooker. Cook on Low 4–5 hours.

Serving suggestion:

Serve chilled.

Variation:

Add 1 pint sliced strawberries about 30 minutes before removing from heat.

Strawberry Rhubarb Sauce

Tina Snyder, Manheim, PA

Makes 8 servings

Prep. Time: 15 minutes   ❧   Cooking Time: 4½–6½ hours   ❧   Ideal slow-cooker size: 3-qt.

6 cups chopped rhubarb

¾ cup sugar

1 cinnamon stick

½ cup white grape juice

pinch salt

2 cups chopped fresh strawberries

1. In slow cooker, stir together rhubarb, sugar, cinnamon stick, grape juice, and salt.

2. Cover and cook on Low for 4–6 hours, until rhubarb is tender.

3. Stir in strawberries and cook 30 minutes longer.

4. Remove cinnamon stick. Chill.

Good go-alongs with this recipe:

Serve as a sauce over pudding, angel food cake, or ice cream.

Fruit Compote Dessert

Beatrice Orgish, Richardson, TX

Makes 8 servings

Prep. Time: 15 minutes ❧ Cooking Time: 3–4 hours ❧ Ideal slow-cooker size: 3½-qt.

2 medium tart apples, peeled

2 medium fresh peaches, peeled and cubed

2 cups unsweetened pineapple chunks

1¼ cups unsweetened pineapple juice

¼ cup honey

2 ¼-inch-thick lemon slices

3½-inch cinnamon stick

1 medium firm banana, thinly sliced

1. Cut apples into ¼-inch slices and then in half horizontally. Place in slow cooker.

2. Add peaches, pineapple, pineapple juice, honey, lemon, and cinnamon. Cover and cook on Low 3–4 hours.

3. Stir in banana slices just before serving.

Serving suggestion:

Garnish with whipped cream, sliced almonds, and maraschino cherries, if you wish.

Festive Strawberry Loaf

Phyllis Good, Lancaster, PA

Makes 1 loaf

Prep. Time: 20 minutes ❧ *Cooking Time: 3½–4 hours* ❧ *Ideal slow-cooker size: 6-qt. oval*

1 cup all-purpose flour

½ cup whole wheat flour

¾ cup sugar

½ tsp. baking soda

¼ tsp. salt

½ tsp. cinnamon

2 eggs

½ cup plus 2 Tbsp. vegetable oil

1 cup chopped fresh, or frozen and thawed, strawberries

Frosting:

4 oz. cream cheese, softened

½ tsp. vanilla extract

4 Tbsp. (½ stick) butter, softened

1¼ cups confectioners' sugar

chopped pecans, *optional*

1. In a large bowl, combine both flours, sugar, baking soda, salt, and cinnamon. When well mixed, form a well in the center of the mixture.

2. In a separate bowl, beat eggs and vegetable oil. Add strawberries. Pour into well in dry ingredients and stir gently just until mixed.

3. Pour into well-greased 8x4-inch loaf pan or whatever size fits in your slow cooker.

4. Place pan into inner crock on top of a small trivet or metal jar lid. Prop lid open at one end with a chopstick or wooden spoon handle.

5. Cook for 3½–4 hours on High, or until toothpick inserted in middle of loaf comes out clean. The top of the loaf may not look set because it won't brown the way it would in the oven, so be sure to start checking at 3½ hours.

6. Carefully remove hot loaf pan and let bread cool in the pan at least 15 minutes. Run a table knife around the loaf and carefully turn pan upside down to get loaf out.

7. To make the frosting, beat cream cheese, vanilla, and butter together until creamy in a medium-sized bowl. Stir in confectioners' sugar.

8. Spread frosting over top and part of the way down the sides of the cooled bread. Sprinkle evenly with pecans if you're using them and press in lightly.

Lemon Bread

Ruth Ann Gingrich, New Holland, PA

Makes 6 servings

Prep. Time: 15 minutes ⚘ *Cooking Time: 2–2¼ hours* ⚘ *Ideal slow-cooker size: 4-qt.*

½ cup shortening
¾ cup sugar
2 eggs, beaten
1⅔ cups flour
1⅔ tsp. baking powder
½ tsp. salt
½ cup milk
½ cup chopped nuts
grated peel from 1 lemon

Glaze:
¼ cup powdered sugar
juice of 1 lemon

1. Cream together shortening and sugar. Add eggs. Mix well.

2. Sift together flour, baking powder, and salt. Add flour mixture and milk alternately to shortening mixture.

3. Stir in nuts and lemon peel.

4. Spoon batter into well-greased 2-pound coffee can and cover with well-greased tinfoil. Place in cooker and set on High for 2–2¼ hours, or until done. Remove bread from coffee can.

5. Mix together powdered sugar and lemon juice. Pour over loaf.

Serving suggestion:
Serve plain or with cream cheese.

Poppy Seed Tea Bread

Julie Hurst, Leola, PA

Makes 10 servings

Prep. Time: 30 minutes ♣ Cooking Time: 3–4 hours
Standing Time: 30 minutes ♣ Ideal slow-cooker size: 6-qt. oval

½ cup whole wheat flour

1½ cups all-purpose flour

¾ cup sugar

2 tsp. baking powder

¼ tsp. salt

¼ cup poppy seeds

2 eggs, room temperature

8 Tbsp. (1 stick) salted butter, melted

¾ cup whole milk, room temperature

½ tsp. almond extract

½ tsp. vanilla extract

TIP
Serve with pineapple whipped cream cheese and tea.

1. In a mixing bowl, combine flours, sugar, baking powder, salt, and poppy seeds.

2. Separately, whisk together eggs, butter, milk, and extracts.

3. Pour wet ingredients into flour mixture, stirring until just combined.

4. Make sure your loaf pan fits in your oval 6-qt. slow cooker. Grease and flour loaf pan. Set it on a jar ring or trivet to keep it off the floor of the cooker.

5. Pour batter into prepared loaf pan.

6. Put lid on cooker, propping it open at one end with a chopstick or wooden spoon handle.

7. Cook on High for 3–4 hours, until tester inserted in middle comes out clean.

8. Wearing oven mitts (to protect your knuckles!), remove hot pan from hot cooker and allow it to cool for 10 minutes. Run a knife around the edge and turn loaf out on cooling rack to cool for an additional 20 minutes before slicing.

Zucchini Bread

Esther J. Yoder, Hartville, OH

Makes 10 servings

Prep. Time: 25 minutes ⚬ Cooking Time: 4 hours
Standing Time: 40 minutes ⚬ Ideal slow-cooker size: 6-qt. oval

2 eggs

2 cups shredded zucchini

1 cup brown sugar

⅔ cup oil

1 tsp. vanilla extract

1 cup chopped walnuts, *optional*

8-oz. pkg. cream cheese, softened

1½ cups whole wheat flour

½ cup rolled oats

1 tsp. baking powder

1 tsp. baking soda

1½ tsp. ground cinnamon

½ tsp. nutmeg

1 tsp. salt

1. Mix eggs, zucchini, sugar, oil, vanilla, and nuts. Mix in cream cheese until smooth.

2. Separately, mix flour, oats, baking powder, baking soda, cinnamon, nutmeg, and salt.

3. Combine wet and dry ingredients, mixing gently until just combined.

4. Make sure you have a loaf pan that fits in your oval 6-qt. cooker. Set it on a jar lid or other heatproof object so the pan is not sitting on the floor of the insert.

5. Grease and flour loaf pan. Pour batter into prepared pan and place in cooker.

6. Prop lid open at one end with a chopstick or wooden spoon handle. Cook on High for 3–4 hours, until tester inserted in middle comes out clean.

7. Wearing oven mitts to protect your knuckles, remove hot pan and allow to sit for 10 minutes. Run knife around edges and turn loaf out to cool for 30 more minutes before slicing.

You Won't Miss the Gluten Cornbread

Hope Comerford, Clinton Township, MI

Makes 10 servings

Prep. Time: 30 minutes ⚬ *Cooking Time: 3–4 hours*
Standing Time: 20 minutes ⚬ *Ideal slow-cooker size: 6-qt. oval*

1 cup gluten-free bread flour
1 cup ground cornmeal
3 tsp. baking powder
3 Tbsp. sugar
1 tsp. salt
2 eggs
⅔ cup milk
⅓ cup melted coconut oil

1. In a bowl, mix together the gluten-free flour, cornmeal, baking powder, sugar, and salt.

2. Briskly whisk in the eggs, milk, and melted coconut oil.

4. Make sure your loaf pan fits in your oval 6-qt. slow cooker. Spray it with nonstick spray. Set it on a jar ring or trivet to keep it off the bottom of the crock.

5. Pour the batter into the prepared loaf pan.

6. Put the cover on the slow cooker, but prop it open at one end with a chopstick or wooden spoon handle.

7. Cook on High for 3–4 hours, until a toothpick inserted in the middle comes out clean.

8. Carefully remove the pan from the crock. Run a knife around the edge and turn loaf out on cooling rack to cool for 10 minutes before slicing.

Sweet Cornbread

Hope Comerford, Clinton Township, MI

Makes 6 servings

Prep. Time: 10 minutes ❧ *Cooking Time: 3½–4 hours* ❧ *Ideal slow-cooker size: 3-qt.*

1 cup cornmeal

1 cup flour

⅔ cup sugar

2 tsp. baking powder

3 Tbsp. butter, melted

¼ cup vegetable oil

1 egg

1–2 Tbsp. honey

1 cup milk

¼ cup frozen corn, *optional*

1. In a bowl, mix the cornmeal, flour, sugar, and baking powder.

2. Next, add the melted butter, vegetable oil, egg, honey, and milk and mix it up.

3. Add the corn (if using) and stir again.

4. Grease your crock with nonstick spray and pour in the batter.

5. Cover and cook on Low for 3½–4 hours.

TIP

If you know your slow cooker really well, you might notice it has a "hot spot" where it tends to cook that spot faster. When making breads or desserts, it's a good idea to cover that hot spot with aluminum foil. It will help keep your bread or dessert from burning in that spot!

Equivalent Measurements

dash = little less than ⅛ tsp.

3 tsp. = 1 Tbsp.

2 Tbsp. = 1 oz.

4 Tbsp. = ¼ cup

5 Tbsp. plus 1 tsp. = ⅓ cup

8 Tbsp. = ½ cup

12 Tbsp. = ¾ cup

16 Tbsp. = 1 cup

1 cup = 8 oz. liquid

2 cups = 1 pt.

4 cups = 1 qt.

4 qt. = 1 gal.

1 stick butter = ¼ lb.

1 stick butter = ½ cup

1 stick butter = 8 Tbsp.

beans, 1 lb. dried = 2–2½ cups (depending on the size of the beans)

bell pepper, 1 large = 1 cup chopped

cheese, hard (for example, cheddar, Swiss, Monterey Jack, mozzarella), 1 lb. grated = 4 cups

cheese, cottage, 1 lb. = 2 cups

chocolate chips, 6-oz. pkg. = 1 scant cup

crackers (butter, saltines, snack), 20 single crackers = 1 cup crumbs

herbs, 1 Tbsp. fresh = 1 tsp. dried

lemon, 1 medium-sized = 2–3 Tbsp. juice

lemon, 1 medium-sized = 2–3 tsp. grated rind

mustard, 1 Tbsp. prepared = 1 tsp. dry or ground mustard

oatmeal, 1 lb. dry = about 5 cups dry

onion, 1 medium-sized = ½ cup chopped

Pasta

macaroni, penne, and other small or tubular shapes, 1 lb. dry = 4 cups uncooked

noodles, 1 lb. dry = 6 cups uncooked

spaghetti, linguine, fettucine, 1 lb. dry = 4 cups uncooked

potatoes, white, 1 lb. = 3 medium-sized potatoes = 2 cups mashed

Potatoes, sweet, 1 lb. = 3 medium-sized potatoes = 2 cups mashed

rice, 1 lb. dry = 2 cups uncooked

sugar, confectioners', 1 lb. = 3½ cups sifted

whipping cream, 1 cup unwhipped = 2 cups whipped

whipped topping, 8-oz. container = 3 cups

yeast, dry, 1 envelope (¼ oz.) = 1 Tbsp.

Recipe and Ingredient Index

F
Fabulous Fajitas, 131
Fajitas
    Fabulous Fajitas, 131
    Italian Chicken Fajita Wraps, 65
Fajita Steak, 129
Fast and Fabulous Brussels Sprouts, 217
Festive Strawberry Loaf, 309
Fish
    flounder
        Herbed Flounder, 177
    Tex-Mex Luau, 175
Flounder
    Herbed Flounder, 177
Fresh Green Beans, 183
Fresh Veggie Lasagna, 159
Fruit Compote Dessert, 307

G
Garlicky Potatoes, 251
German Potato Salad, 249
Ginger
    Beef Roast with Homemade Ginger-Orange
        Sauce, 135
    Green Grape Ginger Tea, 45
Glazed Barbecue Turkey Meatloaf, 85
Gluten-Free Four Berry Cobbler, 259
Gluten-Free Vegetarian Lasagna, 157
Grape jelly
    Sweet 'n Sour Meatballs, 11
Grape juice, white
    Green Grape Ginger Tea, 45
Grapes
    Tapioca Salad, 299
Green Beans with Dill, 185
Green Grape Ginger Tea, 45

H
Ham
    Fresh Green Beans, 183
Heavenly Barbecued Chicken Wings, 51
Herbed Cheese Terrine, 35
Herbed Chicken, 69
Herbed Flounder, 177
Herby Chicken with Pesto, 71

Honey Barbecue Meatballs, 9

I
Italian Chicken Fajita Wraps, 65
Italiano Spread, 37

J
Jalapeño pepper
    Creamy Artichoke Dip, 19
    Marilyn's Chili Con Queso, 25
    Pineapple Jalapeño Chicken, 63
    Salsa Lentils, 167
Jazzed-Up Barbecue Pulled Chicken, 57
Jelly, grape
    Sweet 'n Sour Meatballs, 11
Just Peachy, 277
Just Rice Pudding, 295

L
Lasagna
    Fresh Veggie Lasagna, 159
    Gluten-Free Vegetarian Lasagna, 157
Lemon Bread, 311
Lemon Red Potatoes, 253
Lentils
    Lentil Tacos, 169
    Salsa Lentils, 167
Lettuce
    Italian Chicken Fajita Wraps, 65

M
Macaroni
    "Baked" Macaroni and Cheese, 155
    Creamy Mac and Cheese, 153
Mama's Rice Pudding, 293
Marilyn's Chili Con Queso, 25
Marinated Summer Vegetables, 223
Meatballs
    Chipotle Orange Barbecue Meatballs, 13
    Honey Barbecue Meatballs, 9
    Sweet 'n Sour Meatballs, 11
Mediterranean Eggplant, 205
Memories of Tucson Chicken, 77
Mint
    Basil Mint Tea, 43

About the Author

Hope Comerford is a mom, wife, elementary school music teacher, blogger, recipe developer, public speaker, ALM Zone fit leader, Young Living Essential Oils essential oil enthusiast/educator, and published author. In 2013, she was diagnosed with a severe gluten intolerance and since then has spent many hours creating easy, practical and delicious gluten-free recipes that can be enjoyed by both those who are affected by gluten and those who are not.

Growing up, Hope spent many hours in the kitchen with her Mémé (grandmother) and her love for cooking grew from there. While working on her master's degree when her daughter was young, Hope turned to her slow cookers for some salvation and sanity. It was from there she began truly experimenting with recipes and quickly learned she had the ability to get a little more creative in the kitchen and develop her own recipes.

In 2010, Hope started her blog, *A Busy Mom's Slow Cooker Adventures*, simply to share the recipes she was making with her family and friends. She never imagined people all over the world would begin visiting her page and sharing her recipes with others as well. In 2013, Hope self-published her first cookbook, *Slow Cooker Recipes 10 Ingredients or Less and Gluten-Free*, and then later wrote *The Gluten-Free Slow Cooker*.

Hope became the new brand ambassador and author of Fix-It and Forget-It in mid-2016. She is excited to bring her creativity to the Fix-It and Forget-It brand. Through Fix-It and Forget-It, she has written *Fix-It and Forget-It Lazy & Slow, Fix-It and Forget-It Healthy Slow Cooker Cookbook, Fix-It and Forget-It Favorite Slow Cooker Recipes for Mom, Fix-It and Forget-It Favorite Slow Cooker Recipes for Dad, Fix-It and Forget-It Welcome Home Cookbook, Fix-It and Forget-It Holiday Favorites*, and *Fix-It and Forget-It Cooking for Two*.

Hope lives in the city of Clinton Township, Michigan, near Metro Detroit. She is a native of Michigan and lived there her whole life. She has been happily married to her husband and best friend, Justin, since 2008. Together they have two children, Ella and Gavin, who are her motivation, inspiration, and heart. In her spare time, Hope enjoys traveling, singing, cooking, reading books, spending time with friends and family, and relaxing.